A-Z MAIDSTONE, CHATHAM, GILLINGHAM & ROCHESTER

CW00665818

Reference

Motorway	M20
A Road	A2
Under Construction	
Proposed	
B Road	B2097
Dual Carriageway	
One Way Street — Traffic flow on A roads is indicated by a heavy line on the drivers' left	→
Pedestrianized Road	
Restricted Access	

Track & Footpath	= = = = - -
Residential Walkway	· · · · · · ·
Railway — Tunnel / Level Crossing / Station	
Built Up Area	HIGH STREET
Local Authority Boundary	— · — · —
Posttown Boundary	
Postcode Boundary within Posttown	
Map Continuation	8
Car Park selected	P

Church or Chapel	†
Cycle Route	
Fire Station	■
Hospital	H
House Numbers A & B Roads Only	33 / 2
Information Centre	i
National Grid Reference	160
Police Station	▲
Post Office	★
Toilet	▽
with facilities for the Disabled	♿

Scale 1:19,000
3⅓ inches to 1 mile or 5.26 cm to 1 km

0 — ¼ — ½ — ¾ Mile
0 — 250 — 500 — 750 Metres — 1 Kilometre

Geographers' A-Z Map Company Limited

Head Office : Fairfield Road, Borough Green, Sevenoaks, Kent TN15 8PP Telephone 01732 781000 (General Enquiries & Trade Sales)
Showrooms : 44 Gray's Inn Road, London WC1X 8HX Telephone 020 7440 9500 (Retail Sales)

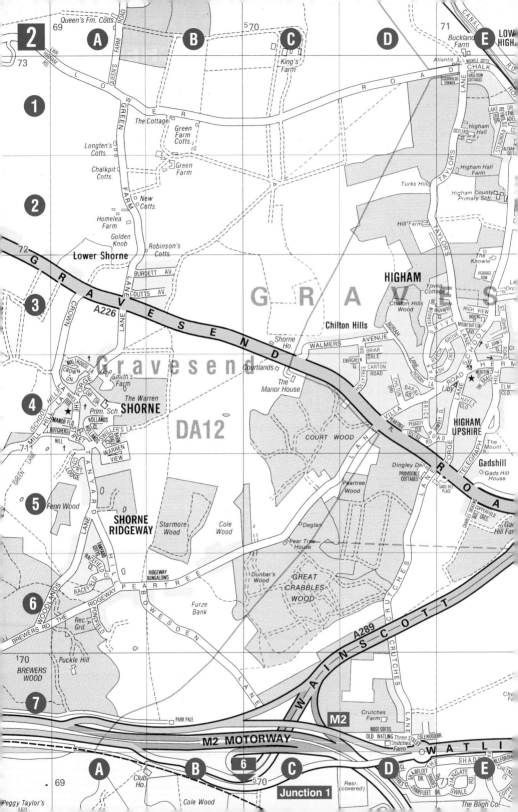

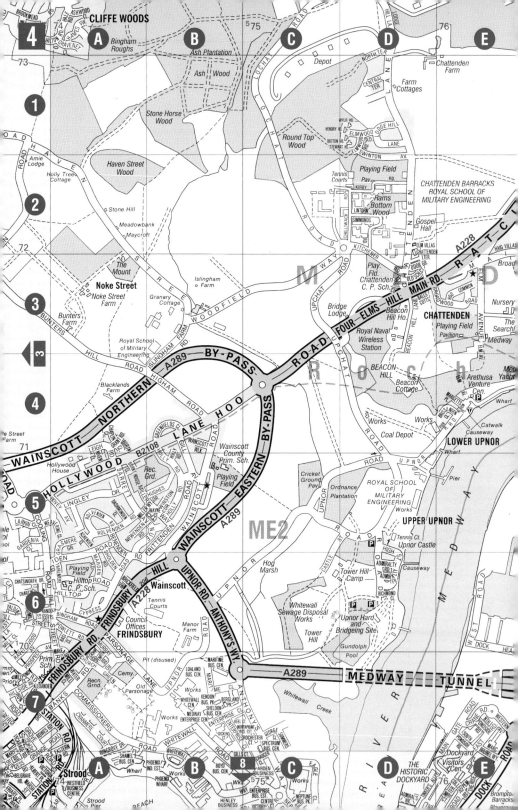

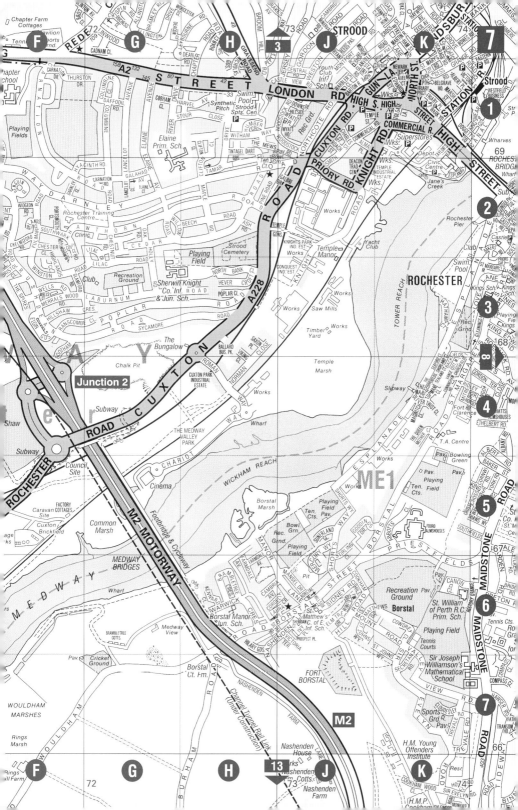

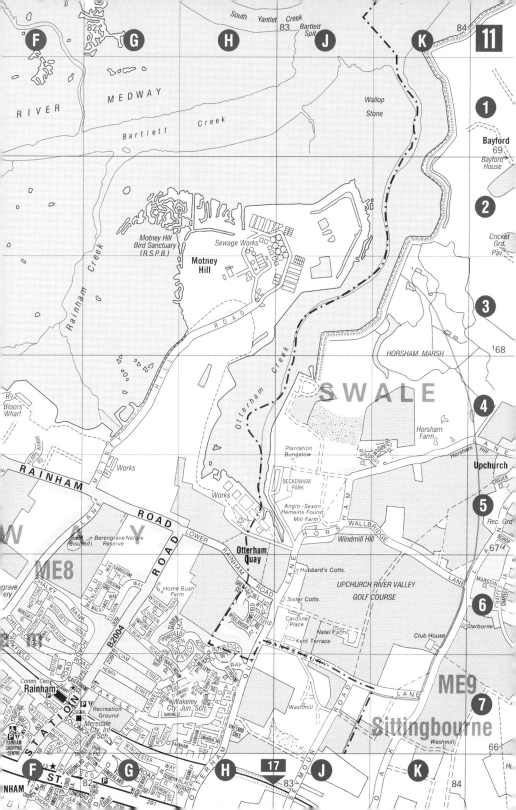

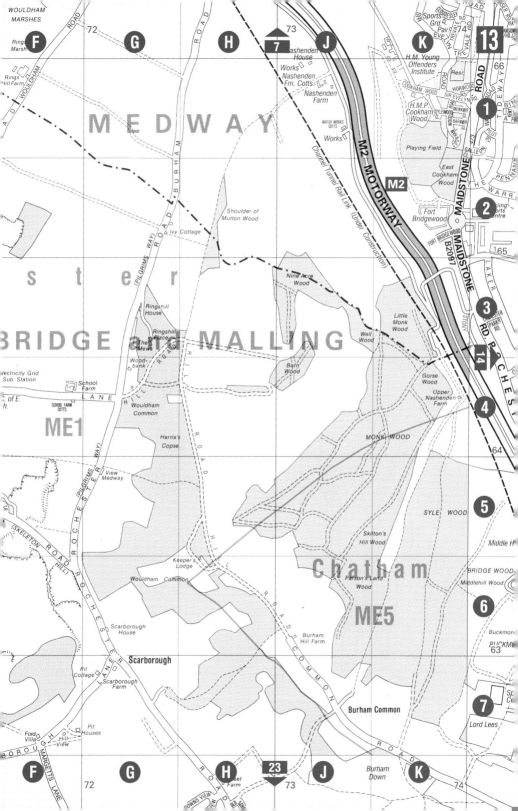

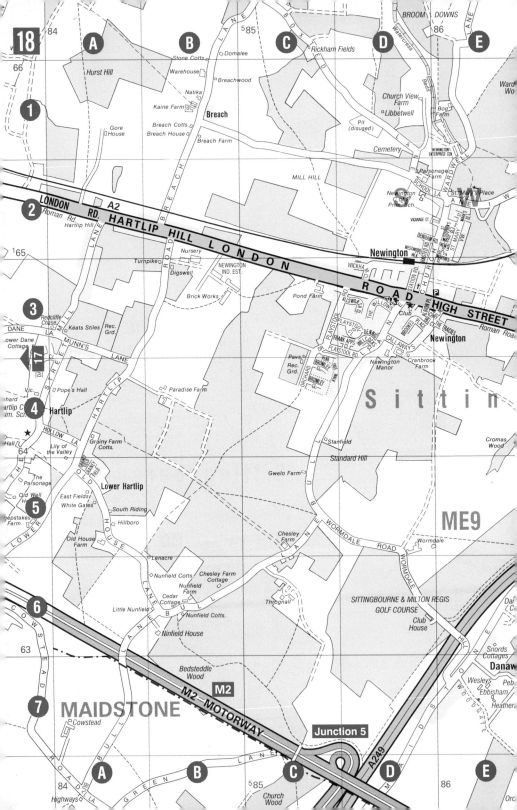

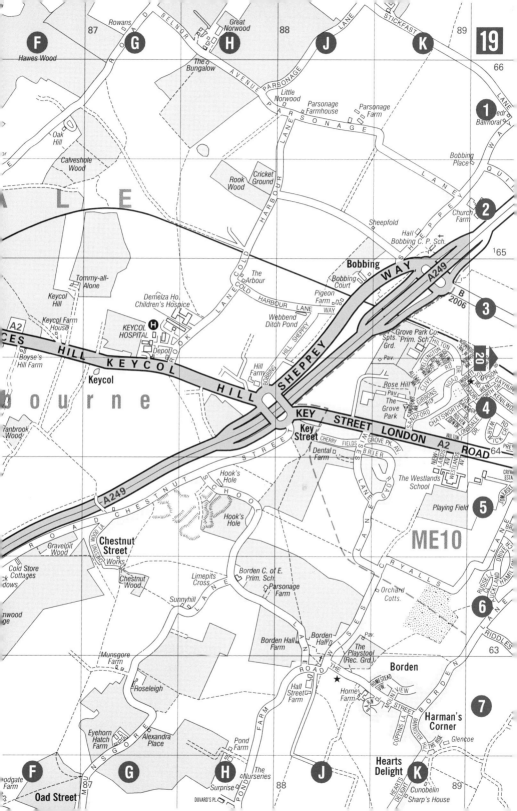

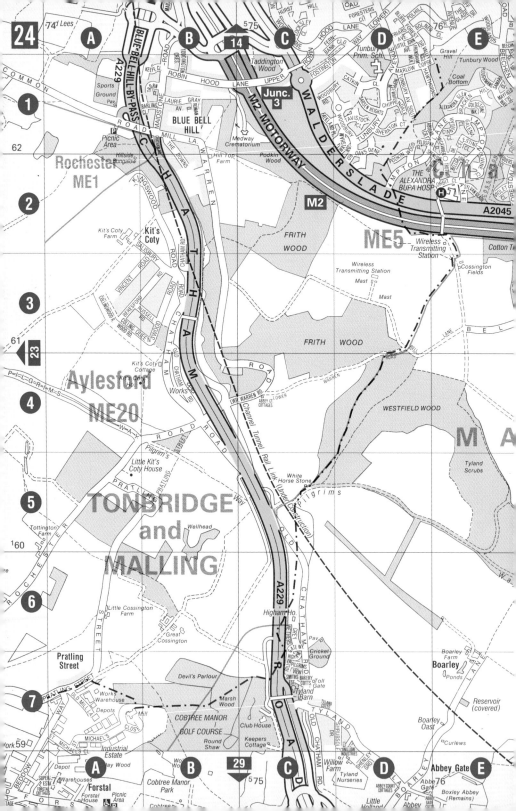

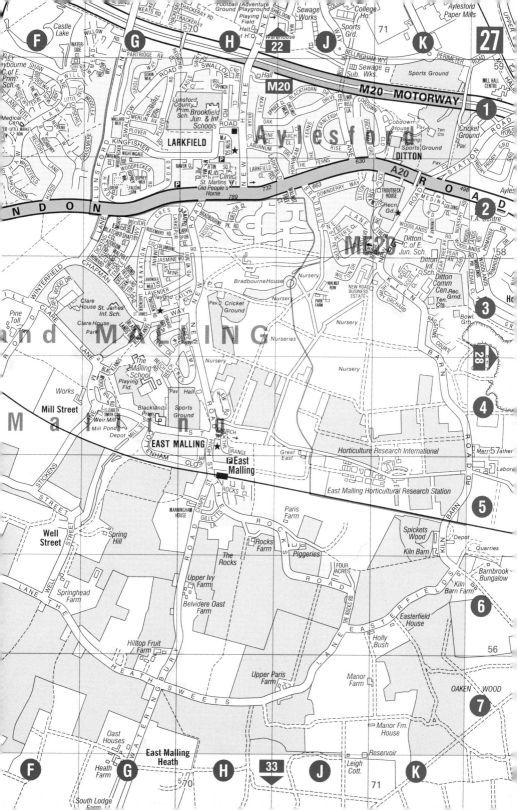

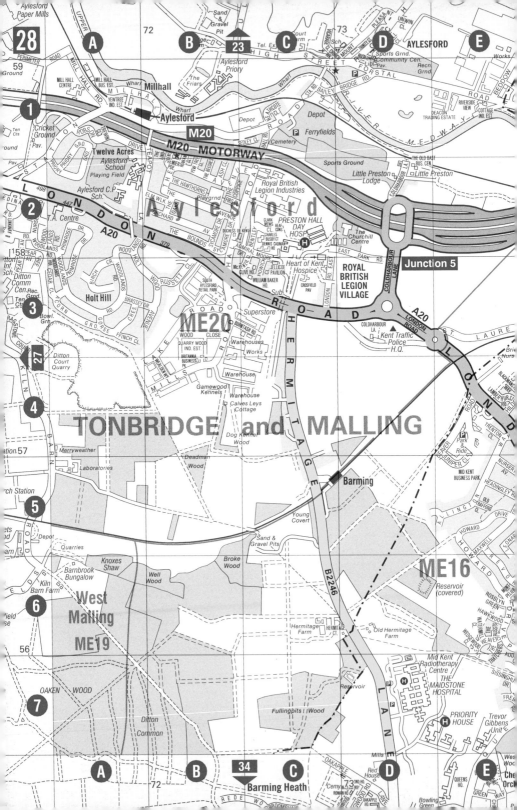

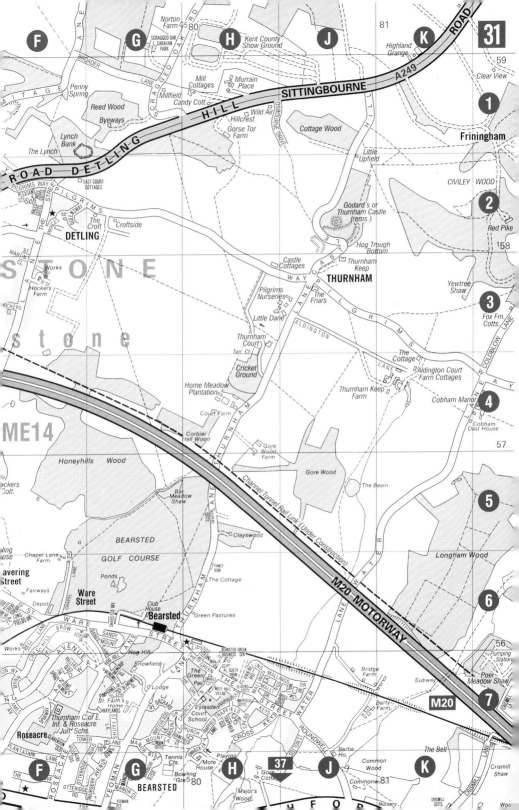

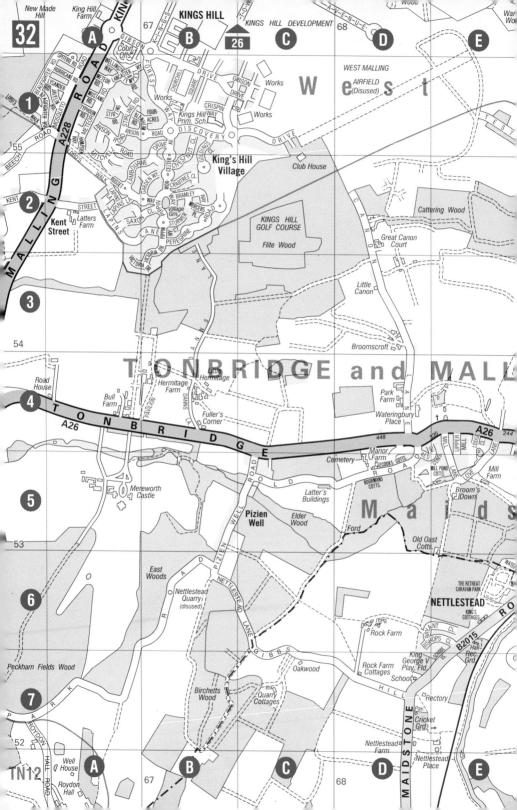

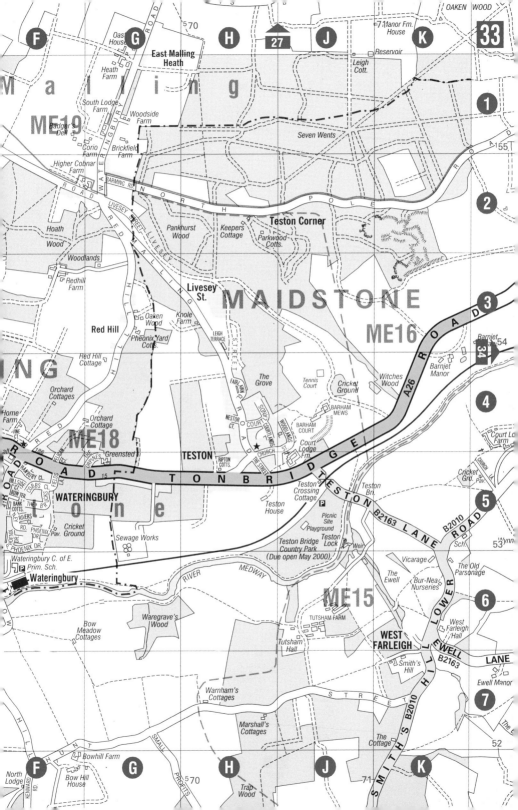

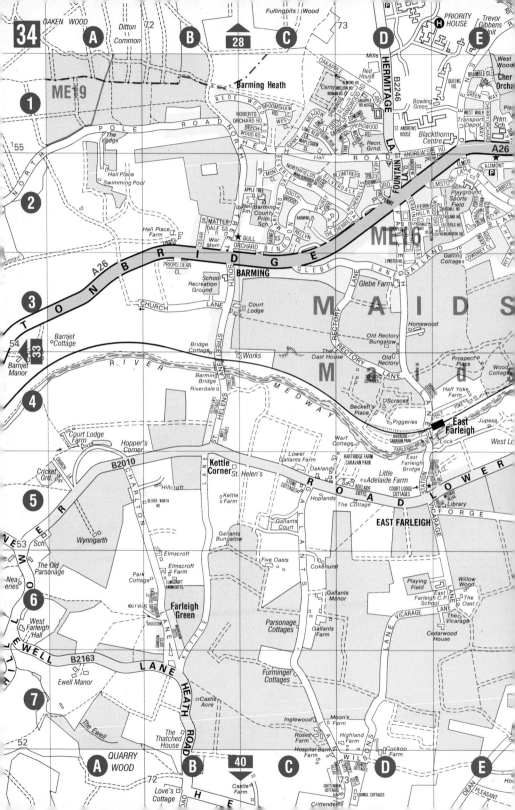

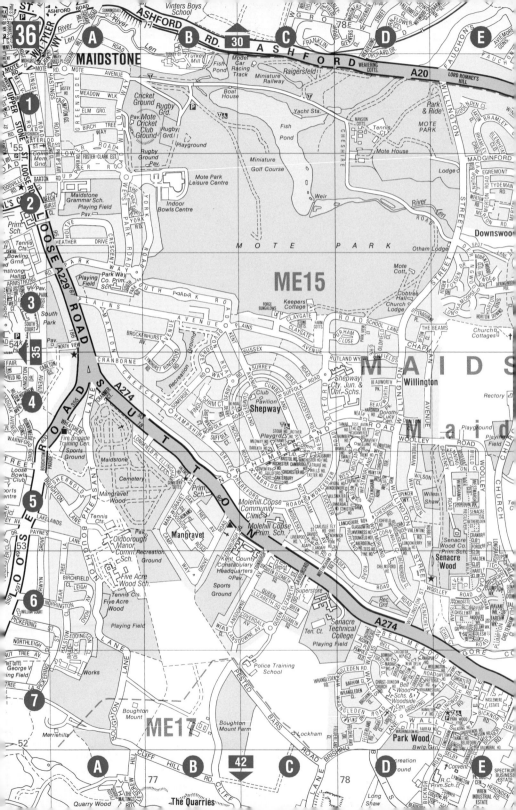

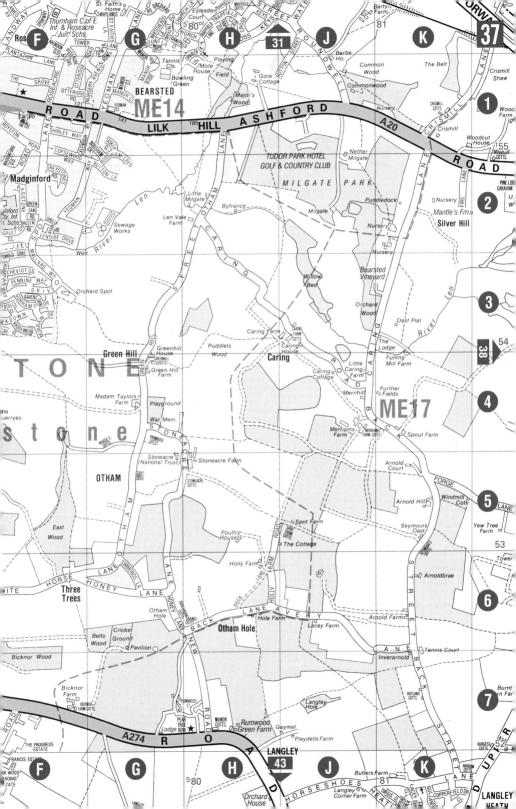

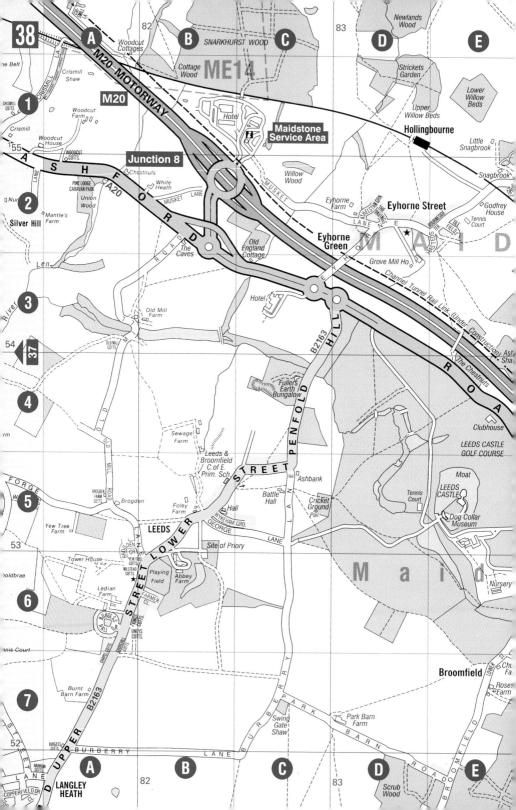

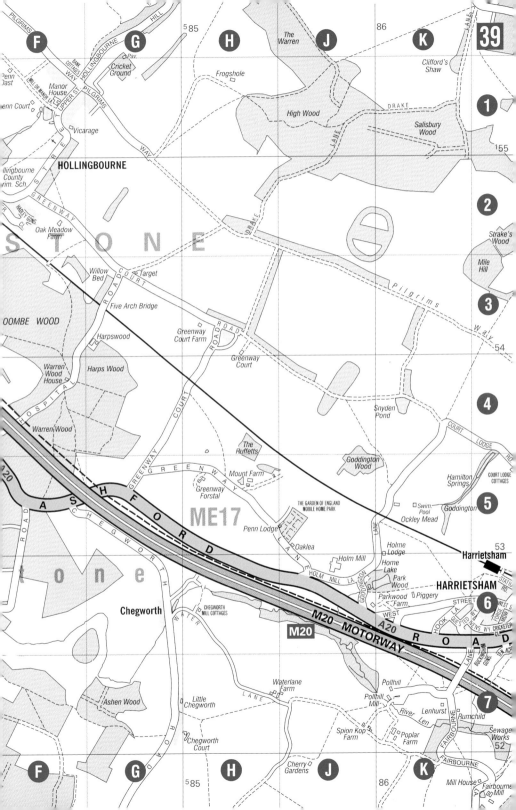

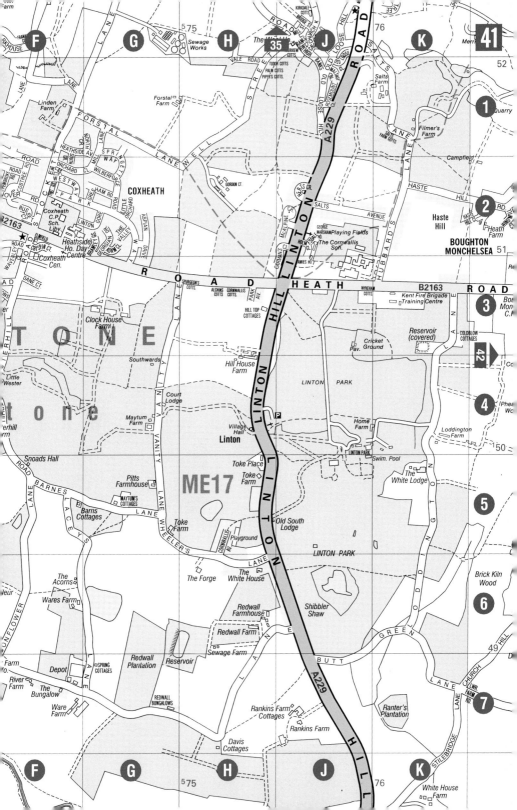

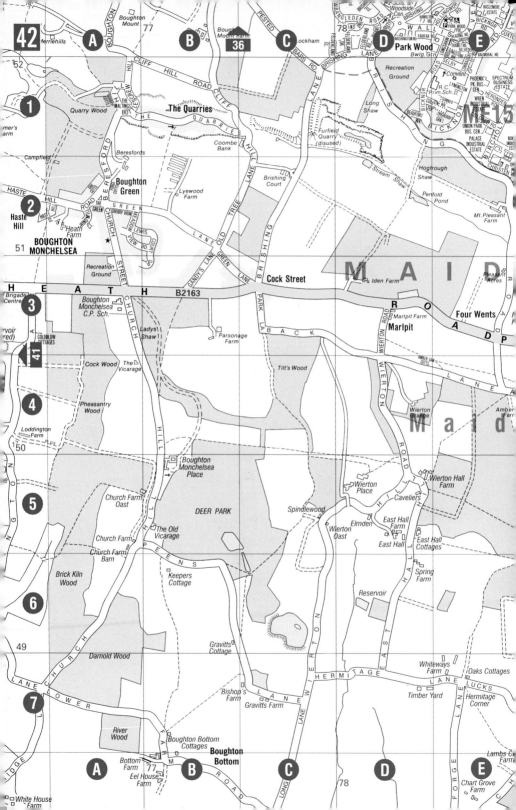

INDEX TO STREETS
Including Industrial Estates and a selection of Subsidiary Addresses.

HOW TO USE THIS INDEX

1. Each street name is followed by its Postal District and then by its map reference; e.g. Abbey Rd. *Roch* —7H **3** is in the Rochester Posttown and is to be found in square 7H on page **3**.
A strict alphabetical order is followed in which Av., Rd., St., etc. (though abbreviated) are read in full and as part of the street name; e.g. Apple Clo. appears after Appleby Clo. but before Appledore Ct.

2. Streets and a selection of Subsidiary names not shown on the Maps, appear in the index in *Italics* with the thoroughfare to which it is connected shown in brackets; e.g. Aintree Ho. *Maid* —6E **36** (off Epsom Clo.)

GENERAL ABBREVIATIONS

All : Alley
App : Approach
Arc : Arcade
Av : Avenue
Bk : Back
Boulevd : Boulevard
Bri : Bridge
B'way : Broadway
Bldgs : Buildings
Bus : Business
Cvn : Caravan
Cen : Centre
Chu : Church

Chyd : Churchyard
Circ : Circle
Cir : Circus
Clo : Close
Comn : Common
Cotts : Cottages
Ct : Court
Cres : Crescent
Dri : Drive
E : East
Embkmt : Embankment
Est : Estate
Gdns : Gardens

Ga : Gate
Gt : Great
Grn : Green
Gro : Grove
Ho : House
Ind : Industrial
Junct : Junction
La : Lane
Lit : Little
Lwr : Lower
Mnr : Manor
Mans : Mansions
Mkt : Market

M : Mews
Mt : Mount
N : North
Pal : Palace
Pde : Parade
Pk : Park
Pas : Passage
Pl : Place
Quad : Quadrant
Rd : Road
Shop : Shopping
S : South
Sq : Square

Sta : Station
St : Street
Ter : Terrace
Trad : Trading
Up : Upper
Vs : Villas
Wlk : Walk
W : West
Yd : Yard

POSTTOWN AND POSTAL LOCALITY ABBREVIATIONS

All : Allington
Ayle : Aylesford
Bap : Bapchild
Barm : Barming
Bear : Bearsted
Blue B : Blue Bell Hill
Bob : Bobbing
B'den : Borden
Bou M : Boughton Monchelsea
Boxl : Boxley
Bred : Bredhurst
Bromp : Brompton
Broom : Broomfield
Burh : Burham
Cha S : Chart Sutton
Chat : Chatham
Chatt : Chattenden
Cli : Cliffe

Cox : Coxheath
Cux : Cuxton
Det : Detling
Dit : Ditton
Down : Downswood
E Far : East Farleigh
E Mal : East Malling
E Peck : East Peckham
Eccl : Eccles
Gill : Gillingham
Gill B : Gillingham Bus. Pk.
Hall : Halling
H'shm : Harrietsham
H'lip : Hartlip
Hem : Hempstead
High : Higham
Holl : Hollingbourne
Hoo : Hoo

Hunt : Hunton
Iwade : Iwade
Kem : Kemsley
King H : Kings Hill
Kgswd : Kingswood
Langl : Langley
Lark : Larkfield
Leeds : Leeds
Leyb : Leybourne
Lin : Linton
Loose : Loose
Lwr Hal : Lower Halstow
Lwr U : Lower Upnor
Maid : Maidstone
Mere : Mereworth
Mil R : Milton Regis
Murs : Murston
Nett : Nettlestead

N'tn : Newington
Otham : Otham
Quar W : Quarry Wood
Rain : Rainham
Roch : Rochester
Roy B : Royal British Legion Village
Rya : Ryarsh
St Mi : St Marys Island
S'lng : Sandling
Shorne : Shorne
Sit : Sittingbourne
Snod : Snodland
S'bry : Stockbury
Strood : Strood
Sut V : Sutton Valence
Tstn : Teston
T'hm : Thurnham

Tonge : Tonge
Tovil : Tovil
Upc : Upchurch
Upnor : Upnor
Up H'lng : Upper Halling
Wain : Wainscott
W'slde : Walderslade
W'bury : Wateringbury
Weav : Weavering
W Far : West Farleigh
W Mal : West Malling
W'sham : Windlesham
Woul : Wouldham
Yald : Yalding

INDEX TO STREETS

Abbeville Ho. *Roch* —4A **8**
Abbey Brewery Ct. *W Mal*
—3D **26**
Abbey Cotts. *S'lng* —2J **29**
Abbey Ct. Cotts. *Chat* —4C **24**
Abbey Ct. Cotts. *S'lng* —1J **29**
Abbey Ga. Cotts. *S'lng* —1J **29**
Abbey Rd. *Gill* —6A **10**
Abbey Rd. *Roch* —7H **3**
Abbey Wood Rd. *King H* —6B **26**
Abbots Ct. Rd. *Hoo* —2K **5**
Abbots Field. *Maid* —2E **34**
Abbotts Clo. *Roch* —5K **7**
Aberdeen Ho. *Maid* —5D **36**
Abigail Cres. *W'slde* —1D **24**
Abingdon Rd. *Chat* —7H **15**
Abinger Dri. *Chat* —7H **15**
Absolam Ct. *Gill* —6C **10**
Acacia Ter. *Sit* —5A **20**
Acadamy Dri. *Gill* —7K **9**
Achilles Rd. *Chat* —7G **15**
Acorn Gro. *Dit* —3A **28**
Acorn Pl. *Maid* —6D **36**
Acorn Rd. *Gill* —4K **9**
Acorn Wharf Rd. *Roch* —2A **8**
Acre Clo. *Chat* —7C **8**
Acre Gro. *Hall* —5C **12**
Adam Clo. *Cox* —2G **41**
Adbert Dri. *E Far* —1E **40**
Addington Rd. *Sit* —6C **20**
Addison Clo. *E Mal* —2G **27**
Adelaide Cotts. *Maid* —5D **34**
Adelaide Dri. *Sit* —5A **20**
Adelaide Rd. *Gill* —4G **9**
Adelaide, The. *High* —1E **2**
Aden Ter. *Maid* —4K **29**
Adisham Dri. *Maid* —4E **28**
Adisham Grn. *Kem* —1D **20**
Admiral Moore Dri. *Roy B*
—2C **28**
Admirals Wlk. *Chat* —6F **15**
(Lords Wood La.)
Admiral's Wlk. *Chat* —1D **8**
(Main Ga. Rd.)

Admiralty Rd. *Upnor* —6D **4**
Admiralty Ter. *Gill* —1E **8**
Admiralty Ter. *Upnor* —6D **4**
Afghan Rd. *Chat* —4C **8**
Aintree Ho. *Maid* —6E **36**
(off Epsom Clo.)
Aintree Rd. *Chat* —6G **15**
Ajax Rd. *Roch* —2A **14**
Alamein Av. *Chat* —2D **14**
Albany Rd. *Chat* —6F **9**
Albany Rd. *Gill* —4H **9**
Albany Rd. *Roch* —4A **8**
Albany Rd. *Sit* —6C **20**
Albany St. *Maid* —6A **30**
Albany Ter. *Chat* —4C **8**
Albany Ter. *Gill* —4H **9**
Albatross Av. *Roch* —1E **6**
Albemarle Rd. *Chat* —7F **15**
Albert Mnr. *Gill* —3F **9**
Albert Pl. *Roch* —1K **7**
Albert Rd. *Chat* —5E **8**
Albert Rd. *Gill* —4G **9**
Albert Rd. *Roch* —4A **8**
Albert St. *Maid* —5J **29**
Albion Pl. *Lwr U* —4E **4**
Albion Pl. *Maid* —7K **29**
Albion Pl. *N'tn* —3D **18**
Albion Rd. *Chat* —7F **15**
Albion Ter. *Sit* —3D **20**
Albury Clo. *Chat* —7H **15**
Alchins Cotts. *Langl* —3H **41**
Aldershot Rd. *Chat* —2E **14**
Aldington Clo. *Chat* —4B **22**
Aldington La. *T'hm* —3J **31**
Aldington Rd. *Bear* —7E **30**
Aldon Clo. *Maid* —2D **14**
Aldon Ct. *Maid* —5B **30**
Alexander Cotts. *High* —1E **2**
Alexander Ct. *Roch* —7K **3**
Alexandra Av. *Gill* —4J **9**
Alexandra Glen. *W'slde* —1E **24**
Alexandra Rd. *Chat* —6F **9**
Alexandra St. *Maid* —5J **29**

Alfred Clo. *Chat* —6F **9**
Alkham Rd. *Maid* —7B **30**
Allenby Wlk. *Sit* —4K **19**
Allen Clo. *Chat* —3G **15**
Allen St. *Maid* —6K **29**
Allington Dri. *Roch* —7G **3**
Allington Gdns. *W'bury* —5E **32**
Allington Rd. *Gill* —5A **10**
Allington Way. *Maid* —5E **28**
Allison Av. *Gill* —7J **9**
Allnutt Mill Clo. *Tovil* —2H **35**
All Saints Rd. *Gill* —5G **21**
Allsworth Clo. *N'tn* —3D **18**
Alma Pl. *Roch* —1J **7**
Alma Rd. *Eccl* —4H **23**
Alma Rd. *W Mal* —3B **26**
Almery Cotts. *Cha S* —5G **43**
Almond Gro. *Hem* —5A **16**
Almond Ho. *Maid* —1D **34**
Almonds, The. *Bear* —7F **31**
Almon Pl. *Roch* —3B **8**
Alton M. *Gill* —4G **9**
Amanda Clo. *Chat* —6D **14**
Amberfield Cotts. *Cha S*
—4F **43**
Amber Grn. Cotts. *Cha S*
—4D **42**
Amber La. *Cha S* —4E **42**
Amber Way. *Cha S* —4G **43**
Ambleside. *Sit* —6G **21**
Ambley Grn. *Gill B* —1A **16**
Ambley Rd. *Gill B* —7A **10**
Ambrose Hill. *Chat* —6G **9**
Ames Av. *Bear* —7F **31**
Amethyst Av. *Chat* —3C **14**
Amherst Clo. *Maid* —7G **29**
Amherst Hill. *Gill* —2E **8**
Amherst Redoubt. *Gill* —3E **8**
Amherst Rd. *Roch* —5B **8**
Amhurst Vs. *Maid* —1C **40**
Amies Ho. *Maid* —5J **29**
Amsbury Rd. *Hunt* —3D **40**
Anchor Bus. Pk. *Sit* —3F **21**

Anchor Rd. *Roch* —7A **8**
Andover Wlk. *Maid* —6E **36**
Andrew Broughton Way. *Maid*
—7A **30**
Andrew Mnr. *Gill* —2F **9**
Andrews Wlk. *Sit* —4K **19**
Anerley Clo. *Maid* —4G **29**
Anglesey Av. *Maid* —6K **35**
Anglesey Clo. *Chat* —2F **15**
Anne Figg Ct. *Roch* —4A **8**
Annie Rd. *Snod* —4B **22**
Annvera Ho. *Gill* —1G **9**
Ansell Av. *Chat* —6E **8**
Anselm Clo. *Sit* —5C **20**
Anson Clo. *Chat* —3G **15**
Anson Rd. *W Mal* —1A **32**
Anthony's Way. *Roch* —6B **4**
(in two parts)
Appleby Clo. *Roch* —2B **14**
Apple Clo. *Snod* —4B **22**
Appledore Ct. *Maid* —4F **29**
Appledore Rd. *Gill* —5A **10**
Apple Tree Clo. *Barm* —2C **34**
Archer Rd. *Chat* —3F **15**
Archibald Rd. *Maid* —4K **29**
Arden Bus. Pk. *Roch* —1C **8**
Ardenlee Dri. *Maid* —6A **30**
Arden St. *Maid* —2G **9**
Arethusa Rd. *Roch* —1A **14**
Argent Ter. *Chat* —4D **14**
Argyle Clo. *Roch* —1C **14**
Arlott La. *Maid* —5J **29**
Armada Way. *Chat* —5D **8**
Armstrong Rd. *Maid* —3K **35**
Armytage Clo. *Hoo* —3J **5**
Arnhem Dri. *Chat* —2D **14**
Arnolde Clo. *Roch* —1C **8**
Arran Rd. *Maid* —6K **35**
Arthur Rd. *Gill* —1D **16**
Arthur Rd. *Roch* —5B **8**
Arthur St. *Sit* —5C **20**
Arundel Clo. *Chat* —1H **25**
Arundel St. *Maid* —5J **29**
Ascot Clo. *Chat* —7G **15**

Ascot Ho. *Maid* —6E **36**
(off Epsom Clo.)
Ashburnham Rd. *Maid* —3A **30**
Ashby Clo. *Hall* —5C **12**
Ash Clo. *Ayle* —2B **28**
Ash Clo. *Chat* —7G **9**
Ash Clo. *Gill* —5B **10**
Ash Cres. *High* —4E **2**
Ashdown Clo. *Maid* —1G **35**
Ashdowns Cotts. *Maid* —1C **40**
Ashenden Clo. *Main* —5A **4**
Ashford Rd. *Maid & Holl*
—7A **30**
Ash Gro. *Maid* —5F **29**
Ashington Clo. *Sit* —4A **20**
Ashley Rd. *Gill* —6C **10**
Ashmead Clo. *Chat* —6G **15**
Ash Rd. *Roch* —2H **7**
Ashtead Dri. *Bap* —7H **21**
Ashton Way. *King N* —6B **26**
Ashtree Ho. *Sit* —6F **21**
(off Woodberry Dri.)
Ash Tree La. *Chat* —6H **9**
Ashurst Rd. *Maid* —6B **30**
Ashwood Clo. *Cli* —1A **4**
Aspen Way. *Chat* —1C **14**
Aspian Dri. *Cox* —2G **41**
Asquith Rd. *Gill* —3C **16**
Association Wlk. *Roch* —2A **14**
Astey Ho. *Maid* —1A **36**
Astley St. *Maid* —7K **29**
Aston Clo. *Chat* —7E **14**
Athelstan Grn. *Holl* —2D **38**
Athelstan Rd. *Chat* —6D **8**
Atlanta Ct. *Chat* —6B **8**
Attlee Cotts. *Hall* —3C **12**
Attlee Way. *Sit* —1C **20**
Aubretia Wlk. *Sit* —6E **20**
Auckland Dri. *Sit* —6E **20**
Auden Rd. *Lark* —7C **22**
Audley Av. *Gill* —7J **9**
Audley Rd. *Maid* —7E **28**
Augusta Clo. *Gill* —1G **9**

Austell Mnr. Gill —2G **9**
(off Skinner St.)
Austen Way. Lark —6B 22
Austin Clo. Kem —1E 20
Autumn Glade. Chat —2H 25
Aveling Clo. Hoo —1H 5
Aveling Ct. Roch —1K 7
Avenue of Rememberance. Sit
—6C 20
Avenue, The. Ayle —2B 28
Averenches Rd. Bear —6E 30
Averenches Rd. S. Bear —7E 30
Avery Clo. Maid —3J 35
Avery La. Otham —6J 27
Aviemore Gdns. Bear —7E 30
Avington Clo. Maid —3J 35
Avocet Wlk. Chat —7G 15
Avondale Rd. Gill —3H 9
Avon Ho. Maid —4D 36
Aylesford Cres. Gill —5B 10
Aylewyn Gn. Kem —1D 20

Backfields. Roch —4K 7
Back La. Cha S —3C 42
Back La. Maid —6H 37
Back St. Leeds —4J 37
Baden Rd. Gill —1H 9
Bader Cres. Chat —2E 14
Badger Rd. Chat —6C 8
Baffin Clo. Chat —6D 8
Bailey Bri. Rd. Ayle —1C 28
Bailey Ct. Gill —1A 16
Bailey Dri. B —7A 10
Bakenham Ho. Roch —7A 8
Baker La. Sut V —6K 43
Baker St. Burh —1H 23
Baker St. Roch —5A 8
Bakers Wlk. Roch —2A 8
Bakery Cotts. S'Ing —7C 24
Balfour Rd. Chat —6C 8
Ballard Bus. Pk. Roch —3H 7
Ballard Ind. Est. Chat —2G 25
Ballens Rd. Chat —6F 15
Balls Ct. Chatt —3B 4
Balmer Clo. Gill —2D 16
Balmoral Ho. Maid —7E 36
Balmoral Rd. Gill —3G 9
Balmoral Ter. Sit —5B 20
Bangor Rd. Roch —2F 7
Bank Cotts. Holl —1F 39
Bankfields Clo. Gill —7H 11
Banks Cotts. W'bury —5F 33
Bankside. Chat —1F 15
Banks Rd. Roch —7A 4
Bank St. Chat —5F 9
Bank St. Maid —7J 29
Banky Meadow. Maid —1C 34
Banning St. Roch —7K 3
Bannister Hill. B'den —7K 19
Bannister Rd. Maid —4K 29
Barbados Ter. Maid —4K 29
Barberry Av. Chat —4B 14
Barcham Ct. Maid —7J 35
Bardell Ter. Chat —3B 8
Barden Ct. Maid —6A 30
Barfleur Mnr. Maid —2E 8
(off Middle St.)
Barfreston Clo. Maid —2J 35
Bargrove Rd. Maid —6B 30
Barham Clo. Maid —7D 36
Barham Ct. Tstn —4J 33
Barham M. Tstn —4J 33
Barker Rd. Maid —1J 35
Barkers Ct. Sit —5B 20
Barkis Clo. Roch —2B 14
Barleycorn. Leyb —2F 27
Barleycorn Dri. Gill —3E 16
Barleyfields. Weav —7C 30
Barleymow Clo. Chat —3G 15
Barling Clo. Chat —1B 24
Barlow Clo. Gill —4K 9
Barming Pl. Maid —2C 34
Barming Rd. W'bury —2G 33
Barnaby Ter. Roch —6A 8
Barnard Ct. Chat —6E 8
Barn Clo. B'den —7J 19
Barncroft Clo. Weav —7E 30
Barncroft Dri. Hem —5K 15
Barndale Ct. Shorne —4A 2
Barned Ct. Maid —2C 34
Barnes La. Lin —5F 41
Barnfield. Chat —1A 24
Barn Hill. Hunt —4B 40
Barn Hill Cotts. Maid —3K 29
Barnhurst Rd. Maid —3K 29
Barn Meadow. Up H'Ing —5A 12
Barnsole Rd. Gill —4G 9
Barnwood Clo. Roch —1K 13

Baron Clo. Bear —6E 30
Baron Clo. Gill —1J 9
Barrie Dri. Lark —6B 22
Barrier R. Chat —3D 8
Barrington Clo. Chat —4D 14
Barrowfields. Chat —1H 25
Barrow Gro. Sit —6B 20
Bartlett Clo. Chat —1G 25
Barton Rd. Maid —2K 35
Barton Rd. Roch —1J 7
Basi Clo. Roch —6A 4
Basing Clo. Maid —1A 36
Basmere Clo. Maid —5B 30
Bassett Rd. Sit —5B 20
Batchelor St. Chat —4E 8
Bates Clo. Lark —7C 22
Bath Hard. Roch —3B 8
Bayford Rd. Sit —5E 20
Bayswater Dri. Gill —5E 16
Baywell. Leyb —1F 27
Beacon Clo. Gill —2D 16
Beacon Hill. Chat —7G 9
Beacon Hill La. Chatt —3D 4
Beacon Rd. Chat —6G 9
Beaconsfield Av. Gill —3J 9
Beaconsfield Rd. Chat —6D 8
Beaconsfield Rd. Maid —2H 35
Beaconsfield Rd. Sit —6G 21
Beacons, The. Cox —3F 41
Beams, The. Maid —3D 36
Bearstead Rd. Maid —4B 30
Bearsted Clo. Gill —5B 10
Bearsted Grn. Bus. Cen. Bear
—7H 31
Beatty Av. Gill —5K 9
Beatty Rd. Roch —5J 7
Beaufighter Rd. W Mal —1A 32
Beaufort Ct. Roch —2C 8
Beaufort Pk. Roch —3C 8
Beaufort Rd. Roch —6G 3
Beaufort Wlk. Maid —1D 42
Beaulieu Rise. Roch —7B 8
Beaulieu Wlk. Maid —4F 29
Beaumont Rd. Maid —2E 34
Beauvoir Dri. Kem —1E 20
Beauworth Pk. Maid —4D 36
Beaver Rd. Maid —4E 28
Beckenham Dri. Maid —4G 29
Beckenham Pk. Gill —5J 11
Beckley M. Chat —4D 14
Becksbourne Clo. Maid —3K 29
Beckworth Pl. Maid —1E 34
Beddow Way. Ayle —1E 28
Bedford Av. Gill —7D 10
Bedford Pl. Maid —7H 29
Bedgebury Clo. Maid —5B 30
Bedgebury Clo. Roch —1B 14
Bedson Wlk. Gill —7H 11
Bedwin Clo. Roch —2B 14
Beech Dri. Maid —4G 29
Beechen Bank Rd. Chat —7E 14
Beeches, The. Ayle —2B 28
Beeches, The. Chat —5E 14
Beech Gro. High —4D 2
Beech Hurst Clo. Maid —2A 36
Beeching Rd. Chat —6F 15
Beechings Clo. Gill —5C 10
Beechings Ind. Cen. Gill —4B 10
Beechings Way. Gill —4B 10
Beechmore Dri. Chat —7E 14
Beech Rd. E Mal —4G 27
Beech Rd. Mere —2A 32
Beech Rd. Roch —2H 7
Beechwood Av. Chat —6H 9
Beechwood Av. Sit —3C 20
Beechwood Rd. Maid —1C 34
Begonia Av. Gill —6C 10
Beke Rd. Gill —5D 16
Belfast Ho. Maid —5D 36
Belgrave Ho. Roch —1K 7
Belgrave St. Eccl —4H 23
Bell Cres. Burh —2H 23
Bellgrove Ct. Chat —2E 24
Bellingham Way. Lark & Ayle
—6D 22
Bell La. Boxl —6F 31
Bell La. Burh —2H 23
Bell La. Chat —3D 24
Bell La. Dit —1J 27
(in two parts)
Bellmeadow. Maid —6D 36
Bell Rd. Maid —6D 36
Bell Rd. Sit —7C 20
Bell Shop. Cen., The. Sit
—5D 20
Bell's La. Hoo —1H 5
Belmont Clo. Maid —2C 34
Belmont Rd. Gill —4G 9
Belmstone. Sit —6C 20

Belnor Av. Bob —1G 19
Belvedere Ho. Maid —7E 36
Bendon Way. Gill —1D 16
Benedict Clo. Hall —5D 12
Benenden Mnr. Gill —5B 10
Benenden Rd. Wain —5A 4
Bennetts Cotts. Gill —2K 25
Bensted Clo. Hunt —6A 40
Bentley Clo. Chat —7H 15
Bentley Clo. Roy B —2C 28
Bentlif Clo. Maid —6G 29
Berber Rd. Roch —7K 3
Berengrave La. Gill —7E 10
Beresford Av. Chat —4H 9
Beresford Hill. Bou M —2A 42
Beresford Rd. Ayle —3A 24
Beresford Rd. Gill —4H 9
Bergland Pk. Roch —7B 4
Berkeley Clo. Roch —1B 14
Berkeley Ct. Sit —6B 20
Berkeley Mt. Chat —4D 8
Berkshire Clo. Chat —1G 15
Berry St. Sit —5D 20
Berwyn Gro. Maid —6K 35
Best St. Chat —4D 8
Bethersden Ct. Maid —5E 36
Betjeman Clo. Lark —7B 22
Betony Gdns. Weav —6E 30
Betsham Rd. Maid —6E 36
Bettscombe Rd. Gill —2D 16
Beverley Clo. Gill —1F 17
Beverley Rd. Maid —2C 34
Bicknor Farm Cotts. Langl
—7F 37
Bicknor Rd. Maid —7E 36
Biddenden Clo. Bear —1E 36
Bilberry Clo. Weav —6D 30
Bill St. Rd. Roch —6A 4
Bilsington Clo. Chat —4F 15
Bingham Rd. Roch —6J 7
Bingley Rd. Snod —2B 22
Binland Gro. Chat —4B 14
Binnacle Rd. Roch —1A 14
Birch Cres. Ayle —3A 28
Birch Dri. Chat —1H 25
Birchfield Clo. Maid —6A 36
Birchfields. Chat —6E 14
Birch Gro. Hem —5A 16
Birch Ho. Barm —1D 34
(off Springwood Rd.)
Birch Ho. Sit —5F 21
Birchington Clo. Maid —6B 30
Bircholt Rd. Maid —1E 42
Birch Tree Way. Maid —1A 36
Birchwood Rd. Maid —6F 29
Birkdale Ct. Maid —7F 29
Birkhall Clo. Chat —4E 14
Birling Av. Bear —7E 30
Birling Av. Rain —7D 10
Birling Clo. Maid —7E 30
Birling Rd. Snod —3B 22
Birling Rd. W Mal —2C 26
Birnam Sq. Maid —7H 29
Bishop Ct. Mil R —4C 20
(off St Paul's St.)
Bishop La. Upc —5K 11
Bishopsbourne Grn. Gill —4B 10
Bishops Clo. Nett —6D 32
Bishop's La. Hunt —6A 40
Bishops Wlk. Roch —3B 8
Bishopsway. Maid —7J 29
Black Cotts. Boxl —5H 25
Blacketts Rd. Tonge —3K 21
Blacklands E Mal —4A 4
(in two parts)
Blacklands Dri. E Mal —3G 27
Blackman Clo. Hoo —1H 5
Blackmanstone Way. Maid
—4E 28
Black Rock Gdns. Hem —5B 16
Blacksmith Dri. Weav —6C 30
Blackthorn Av. Chat —6E 14
Blackthorn Dri. Lark —1J 27
Blackthorne Rd. Gill —1H 17
Blake Dri. Lark   6B 22
Blakeney Clo. Bear —7G 31
Blaker Av. Roch —7C 8
Blatchford Clo. E Mal —2G 27
Bleakwood Rd. Chat —4D 14
Blean Rd. Gill —6C 10
Blean Sq. Maid —5B 30
Blendon Rd. Maid —6B 30
Blenheim Av. Chat —6E 14
Blenheim Clo. Bear —1E 36
Blenheim Rd. Sit —7F 21
Blenheim Rd. W Mal —1A 32
Bligh Way. Roch —1E 6
Blind La. Bred —1K 25
Blind La. Det —2K 25

Blockmakers Ct. Chat —6F **9**
Bloomsbury Wlk. Maid —7K **29**
(off Wyatt St.)
Bloors La. Rain —7D 10
(in two parts)
Bloors Wharf Rd. Gill —4E 10
Blowers Wood Gro. Hem
—6B 16
Bluebell Clo. Gill —2K 9
Blue Bell Hill By-Pass. Chat
—1A 24
Blue Boar La. Roch —3A 8
Bluett St. Maid —5K 29
Blythe Clo. Sit —4G 21
Blythe Rd. Maid —7A 30
Boarley Ct. S'Ing —2J 29
Boarley La. S'Ing —2J 29
(in two parts)
Boarley Rd. S'Ing —2J 29
Bobbing Hill. Bob —4H 19
Bockingford Ct. Maid —4J 35
Bockingford Ho. Maid —4J 35
Bockingford La. Maid —4J 35
Bockingford Mill Cotts. Maid
—4J 35
Bodiam Clo. Gill —5C 10
Bodsham Cres. Bear —2G 37
Boley Hill. Roch —2A 8
Bolner Clo. Chat —7D 14
Bombay Ho. Maid —7D 36
Bondfield Rd. E Mal —3G 27
Bond Rd. Gill —5E 16
Bonflower La. Lin —6F 41
Bonflower La. Lin —6F 41
Bonham Dri. Sit —4E 20
Bonnington Grn. Gill —5C 10
Bonnington Rd. Maid —5B 30
Boormans Cotts. W'bury
—5D 32
Bootham Clo. Roch —4F 7
Booth Rd. Chat —6D 8
Borden La. B'den —7K 19
Borough Rd. Gill —4H 9
Borstal M. Roch —6J 7
Borstal Rd. Roch —5J 7
Borstal St. Roch —5J 7
Boston Gdns. Gill —7C 10
Boston Rd. Chat —7G 15
Bottlescrew Hill. Bou M —1A 42
Boughton Clo. Gill —5C 10
Boughton La. Maid —5A 36
Boughton Pde. Maid —5K 35
Boundary Rd. Chat —5B 8
Bounds, The. Ayle —2B 28
Bourncrete Ho. Sit —4E 20
Bourne Gro. Sit —4A 20
Bourneside Ter. Holl —2E 38
Bournewood Clo. Down —3E 36
Bournville Av. Chat —7D 8
Bower Clo. Maid —7H 29
Bower Grn. Chat —1G 25
Bower La. Maid —1H 35
Bower Mt. Rd. Maid —1G 35
Bower Pl. Maid —1H 35
Bower Rd. Maid —7H 29
Bower Ter. Maid —1H 35
Bowesden La. Shorne —6A 2
Bowes Rd. Roch —7K 3
Bow Hill. W'bury & Yald —6F 33
Bowman Clo. Chat —4G 15
Bow Rd. W'bury —6F 33
Bow Ter. W'bury —5F 33
Boxley Clo. Maid —4A 30
Boxley Grange Cotts. Boxl
—5K 25
Boxley Rd. Maid —5K 29
Boxley Rd. W'slde —7E 14
Boxmend Ind. Est. Maid —1E 42
Boyces Hill. N'tn —3E 18
Boyd Bus. Cen. Roch —1B 8
Bracken Ct. Sit —4G 21
Bracken Hill. Chat —1E 24
Bracken Lea. Chat —7G 9
Brackley Clo. Maid —6B 30
Bradbourne Av. Gill —4C 10
Bradbourne La. Dit —4J 27
Bradbourne Pk. Rd. E Mal
—2H 27
Braddick Clo. Maid —6A 36
Bradfields Av. Chat —3D 14
Bradfields Av. W. Chat —3D 14
Bradley Dri. Sit —7C 20
Bradley Rd. Up H'Ing —4A 12
Braes, The. High —4E 2
Brake Av. Chat —4C 14
Bramble Clo. Maid —1E 34
Brambledown. Chat —1F 15
Brambletree Cotts. Roch —6G 7
Brambletree Cres. Roch —6H 7

Bramley Clo. Gill —1H **17**
Bramley Cres. Bear —1E **36**
Bramley Gdns. Cox —2G **41**
Bramley Rise. Roch —7G **3**
Bramley Rd. Snod —2C 22
Bramley Way. King H —2B 32
Bramshott Clo. Maid —5F 29
Bransgore Clo. Gill —7D 16
Brasenose Rd. Gill —5J 9
Brassey Dri. Ayle —3A 28
Brasted Ct. Roch —6J 3
Bray Gdns. Maid —7J 35
Breach La. Lwr Hal —2B 18
Bredgar Clo. Maid —6A 30
Bredgar Rd. Gill —4A 10
Bredhurst Rd. Gill —3B 16
Brenchley Clo. Roch —6B 8
Brenchley Ho. Maid —6J 29
Brenchley Rd. Gill —6B 10
Brenchley Rd. Maid —2J 35
Brenchley Rd. Sit —7D 20
Brendon Av. Chat —6E 14
Brent Clo. Chat —4C 14
Brenzett Clo. Chat —4F 15
Breton Rd. Roch —6A 8
Brett Wlk. Gill —5D 16
Brewers Rd. Shorne —6A 2
Brewer St. Maid —6K 29
Brewery Rd. Sit —3C 20
Briar Clo. Lark —1H 27
Briar Dale. High —3D 2
Briar Fields. Weav —6D 30
Brice Rd. High —4D 2
Brickfields. W Mal —2C 26
Brickfield View. Roch —6A 4
Brickmakers Ind. Est. Gill
—3F 21
Bridge Cotts. E Far —4B 34
(St Helens La.)
Bridge Cotts. E Far —5E 34
(Station Hill)
Bridge Hill. Ayle —2B 28
Bridge Ind. Est. Tovil —2H 35
Bridge Mill Way. Tovil —2G 35
Bridge Rd. Gill —1G 9
Bridge Rd. Roch —5A 8
Bridge St. Loose —7J 35
Bridgewater Pl. Leyb —1F 27
Brier Clo. Chat —1G 15
Brier Rd. Sit —4J 19
Bright Rd. Chat —6F 9
Brindle Way. Chat —1G 25
Brisbane Av. Sit —5A 20
Brisbane Rd. Chat —5E 8
Brishing Clo. Maid —7D 36
Brishing La. Bou M —3C 42
Brishing La. Maid —7D 36
Brishing Rd. Maid & Cha S
—1D 42
Brisley's Row. Burh —1H 23
Brissenden Clo. Upnor —4E 4
Bristol Clo. Roch —3F 7
Bristol Ho. Maid —5C 36
Britannia Bus. Pk. Quar W
—4B 28
Britannia Clo. Hall —5C 12
Britannia Clo. Sit —2C 20
Britton Farm Rd. Gill —2G 9
Britton St. Gill —3F 9
(in two parts)
Broader La. Det —1G 31
Broadfield Rd. Maid —4K 35
Broadlands Dri. Chat —5F 15
Broadoak. Leyb —1E 26
Broadoak Av. Maid —5K 35
Broad St. Sut V —6K 43
Broadwater Rd. W Mal —6E 26
Broadway. Gill —5A 10
Broadway. Maid —1J 35
Broadway Shop. Cen. Maid
—7J 29
Broadwood Rd. Chatt —3E 4
Brockenhurst Av. Maid —3A 36
Brockenhurst Clo. Gill —2C 16
Brogden Cres. Leeds —6A 38
Brogden Farm Cotts. Loods
—5A 38
Bromley Clo. Chat —5F 15
(in two parts)
Bromley Clo. N'tn —4C 18
(in two parts)
Brompton Clo. Chat —2D 8
Brompton Farm Rd. Roch
—6H 3
Brompton Hill. Chat —2D 8
Brompton La. Roch —7J 3
Brompton Rd. Gill —2F 9
Bronington Clo. Chat —4E 14

Bronte Clo.—Clifton Rd.

Bronte Clo. *Lark* —7B **22**
Brookbank. *Maid* —3K **29**
Brooker's Pl. *High* —1E **2**
Brookes Pl. *N'tn* —3D **18**
Brookfield Av. *Lark* —6C **22**
Brooklands Rd. *Lark* —6C **22**
Brook La. *Snod* —4B **22**
Brooklyn Paddock. *Gill* —2H **9**
Brookmead Rd. *Cli* —1K **3**
Brook Rd. *Lark* —6A **22**
Brookside. *Hoo* —2J **5**
Brooks Pl. *Maid* —7K **29**
Brook St. *Snod* —2D **22**
Brook, The. *Chat* —3D **8**
Broomcroft Rd. *Gill* —6F **11**
Broomfield Rd. *Kgswd* —7E **38**
Broom Hill Rd. *Roch* —7H **3**
Broom Rd. *Sit* —4G **21**
Broomshaw Rd. *Maid* —1C **34**
Browndens Rd. *Up H'lng* —5A **12**
Brownelow Copse. *W'slde* —1E **24**
Brownhill Clo. *Chat* —5E **14**
Browning Clo. *Lark* —6B **22**
Brown St. *Rain* —7E **10**
Brucks, The. *W'bury* —5F **33**
Bruges Ct. *Kem* —1D **20**
Brunswick St. *Maid* —1K **35**
Brunswick St. E. *Maid* —1K **35**
Bryant Clo. *Nett* —6D **32**
Bryant Rd. *Roch* —7J **3**
Bryant St. *Chat* —5E **8**
Buckingham Gdns. *H'shm* —7K **39**
Buckingham Rd. *Gill* —3H **9**
Buckingham Row. *Maid* —5D **36**
Buckland Clo. *Chat* —7E **14**
Buckland Hill. *Maid* —6H **29**
Buckland La. *Maid* —5G **29** (in two parts)
Buckland Pl. *Maid* —7H **29**
Buckland Rd. *Maid* —6H **29**
Buglehorn Cotts. *Maid* —6G **37**
Bulldog Rd. *Chat* —7F **15**
Buller Rd. *Chat* —6D **8**
Bullfields. *Snod* —2C **22**
Bull La. *Eccl* —7H **23**
Bull La. *High* —1F **3**
Bull La. *Roch* —2A **8**
Bull La. *S'bry* —7A **18**
Bull Orchard. *Maid* —2C **34**
Bulrush Clo. *Chat* —6D **14**
Bumbles Clo. *Roch* —1B **14**
Bungalows, The. *Hoo* —2H **5**
Bunters Hill Rd. *Cli* —2J **3**
Burberry La. *Leeds* —7A **38**
Burdett Av. *Shorne* —3A **2**
Burgess Cotts. *Leeds* —7A **38**
Burgess Hall Dri. *Leeds* —6A **38**
Burgess Rd. *Roch* —1K **7**
Burghclere Dri. *Maid* —2E **34**
Burgoyne Ct. *Maid* —4J **29**
Burham Rd. *Roch* —2G **13**
Burham St. *Burh* —1F **23**
Burial Ground La. *Maid* —2H **35**
Burkestone Clo. *Kem* —1E **20**
Burleigh Clo. *Roch* —7G **3**
Burleigh Dri. *Maid* —2J **29**
Burley Rd. *Sit* —5C **20**
Burlington Gdns. *Gill* —5E **16**
Burma Way. *Chat* —3D **14**
Burnham Clo. *Mil R* —1C **20**
Burnham Wlk. *Gill* —6E **16** (in two parts)
Burn Meadow Cotts. *Boxl* —7G **25**
Burns Rd. *Gill* —1G **9**
Burns Rd. *Maid* —2F **35**
Burntash Rd. *Quar W* —3B **28**
Burnt Ho. Clo. *Wain* —5A **4**
Burnt Oak Ter. *Gill* —2G **9**
Burnup Bank. *Sit* —4G **21**
Burritt M. *Roch* —5A **8**
Burrs, The. *Sit* —6E **20**
Burrstock Way. *Rain* —7H **11**
Burston Rd. *Cox* —3E **40**
Burton Clo. *Wain* —4A **4**
Busbridge Rd. *Loose* —6H **35**
Busbridge Rd. *Snod* —3A **22**
Bushmeadow Rd. *Gill* —6F **11**
Bush Rd. *Cux* —5C **6**
Bush Row. *Ayle* —7J **23**
Butchers Hill. *Shorne* —4A **2**
Buttermere Clo. *Gill* —3K **9**
Butt Grn. La. *Lin* —7J **41**
Butt Law Clo. *Hoo* —2J **5**
Button Ho. *Chatt* —1C **4**
Button La. *Bear* —2G **37**
Butts, The. *Sit* —5D **20**
Buxton Clo. *Chat* —1H **25**
Buxton Clo. *Maid* —4K **35**
Bychurch Pl. *Maid* —1K **35**
Byron Rd. *Gill* —5G **9**
Byron Rd. *Maid* —4A **30**
Bythorne Ct. *Rain* —7H **11**

Cadnam Clo. *Roch* —7G **3**
Caernarvon Dri. *Maid* —3J **35**
Calcutta Ho. *Maid* —7D **36**
Caldecote Clo. *Rain* —7H **11**
Calder Rd. *Maid* —4H **29**
Caldew Av. *Gill* —7C **10**
Caldew Gro. *Sit* —6F **21**
Caledonian Ct. *Gill* —1E **16**
Calehill Clo. *Maid* —5B **30**
Callams Clo. *Gill* —3D **16**
Callaways La. *N'tn* —3D **18**
Callis Way. *Gill* —4D **16**
Camborne Mnr. *Gill* —2G **9**
Cambria Av. *Roch* —6H **7**
Cambridge Cres. *Maid* —5C **36**
Cambridge Ho. *Maid* —5C **36**
Cambridge Rd. *Gill* —3C **16**
Cambridge Rd. *Roch* —7J **3**
Cambridge Rd. *Sit* —7F **21**
Cambridge Ter. *Chat* —4D **8**
Camden Clo. *Chat* —4F **15**
Camden Rd. *Gill* —1H **9**
Camden St. *Maid* —6K **29**
Camellia Clo. *Gill* —2D **16**
Cameron Clo. *Chat* —1F **15**
Camomile Dri. *Weav* —6E **30**
Campbell Rd. *Maid* —1K **35**
Camperdown Mnr. Gill —2E 8 (off River St.)
Campion Clo. *Chat* —6C **14**
Campleshon Rd. *Gill* —4D **16**
Campus Way. *Gill B* —1A **16**
Camp Way. *Maid* —5B **36**
Canada Ter. *Maid* —4K **29**
Canadian Av. *Gill* —4J **9**
Canal Rd. *High* —1E **2**
Canal Rd. *Strood* —1A **8**
Canberra Gdns. *Sit* —5A **20**
Canning St. *Maid* —5K **29**
Canon Clo. *Roch* —6K **7**
Canon La. *W'bury* —2D **32**
Canterbury Ho. *Maid* —5C **36**
Canterbury La. *Gill* —6H **11**
Canterbury Rd. *Sit* —6F **21** (in two parts)
Canterbury St. *Gill* —3G **9**
Cape Cotts. *Maid* —7J **35**
Capel Clo. *Gill* —5C **16**
Capell Clo. *Cox* —2F **41**
Capel Rd. *Sit* —7C **20**
Capetown Ho. *Maid* —7E **36**
Capstone Rd. *Chat* —7G **9**
Captain's Clo. *Sut V* —7K **43**
Cardine Clo. *Sit* —2C **20**
Caring Farm Cotts. *Leeds* —3J **37**
Caring La. *Leeds* —4J **37**
Caring Rd. *Otham & Leeds* —2H **37**
Carisbrooke Dri. *Maid* —6G **29**
Carisbrooke Rd. *Roch* —6G **3**
Carlisle Clo. *Roch* —2E **6**
Carlisle Ho. *Maid* —5C **36**
Carlton Av. *Gill* —4J **9**
Carlton Cres. *Chat* —1H **15**
Carlton Gdns. *Maid* —4K **35**
Carman's Clo. *Loose* —3J **41**
Carnatation Clo. *E Mal* —2H **27**
Carnation Cres. *E Mal* —3G **27**
Carnation Dri. *Roch* —1F **7**
Carnation Rd. *Roch* —1F **7**
Caroline Cres. *Maid* —4G **29**
Carpeaux Clo. *Chat* —4E **8**
Carpenters Clo. *Roch* —6C **8**
Carpinus Clo. *Chat* —1F **25**
Carrington Clo. *Gill* —2K **9**
Carroll Gdns. *Lark* —7B **22**
Carton Clo. *Roch* —6B **8**
Carton Rd. *High* —4D **2**
Carvoran Way. *Gill* —4C **16**
Castleacres Ind. Est. *Sit* —3F **21**
Castle Av. *Roch* —4A **8**
Castle Dean. *Maid* —3H **29**
Castle Hill. *Det* —3J **31**
Castle Hill. *Roch* —2A **8**
Castlemaine Av. *Gill* —2K **9**
Castle Rd. *All* —5F **29**
Castle Rd. *Chat* —6E **8**
Castle Rd. *Sit* —5E **20**
Castle Rd. Bus. Precinct. *Sit* —4F **21**
Castle Rd. Technical Cen. *Sit* —4F **21**
Castle Rough La. *Kem* —1D **20**
Castle St. *Upnor* —6C **4**
Castle St. *Woul* —5E **12**
Castle View Rd. *Roch* —1H **7**
Castle Way. *Leyb* —2E **26**
Catherine Clo. *Barm* —1D **34**
Catherine St. *Roch* —5B **8**
Catkin Clo. *Chat* —1D **24**
Catlyn Clo. *E Mal* —3H **27**
Catterick Rd. *Chat* —7H **15**
Cave Hill. *Maid* —3H **35**
Cavell Way. *Sit* —4B **20**
Cavendish Av. *Gill* —2J **9**
Cavendish St. *Roch* —5B **8**
Cavendish Way. *Bear* —1F **37**
Caversham Clo. *Rain* —7F **11**
Cazeneuve St. *Roch* —3A **8**
Cecil Av. *Gill* —6A **10**
Cecil Av. *Roch* —7K **3**
Cecil Rd. *Roch* —5A **8**
Cedar Clo. *Dit* —3A **28**
Cedar Clo. *Sit* —7F **21**
Cedar Ct. *Maid* —6A **30**
Cedar Dri. *Barm* —2B **34**
Cedar Gro. *Hem* —4A **16**
Cedar Rd. *Roch* —2G **7**
Cedars, The. *Sit* —4G **21**
Celestine Clo. *Chat* —1E **24**
Cemetery Cotts. *Maid* —5B **36**
Cemetery Rd. *Hall* —4C **12**
Cemetery Rd. *Snod* —1B **22**
Central Av. *Chat* —7F **5**
Central Av. *Sit* —6D **20**
Central Bus. Pk. *Roch* —1C **8**
Central Pde. *Roch* —6B **8**
Central Pk. Gdns. *Chat* —6C **8**
Central Rd. *Lark* —7D **22**
Central Rd. *Roch* —1J **7**
Central Ter. *Chatt* —1D **4**
Centre 2000. *Sit* —5E **20**
Centre Ct. *Roch* —1C **8**
Centurion Clo. *Gill B* —7K **9**
Century Building. *Roch* —3A **8**
Century Rd. *Gill* —1D **16**
Ceres Ct. *Sit* —4G **21**
Chada Av. *Gill* —5J **9**
Chaffe's La. *Upc* —6K **11**
Chaffes Ter. *Upc* —6K **11**
Chaffinch Clo. *Chat* —2E **14**
Chalfont Dri. *Gill* —3D **16**
Chalgrove M. *Hall* —4C **12**
Chalkenden Av. *Gill* —6A **10**
Chalk Pit Hill. *Chat* —5E **8**
Chalk Rd. *High* —1E **2**
Chalkwell Rd. *Sit* —5B **20**
Chalky Bank Rd. *Gill* —6F **11**
Challenger Clo. *Sit* —2C **20**
Challock Wlk. *Maid* —5B **30**
Chamberlain Av. *Maid* —2E **34**
Chamberlain Ct. *Gill* —4B **16**
Chamberlain Rd. *Chat* —6F **9**
Chancery La. *Maid* —1K **35**
Chapel Cotts. *Leeds* —7A **38**
Chapel La. *Bear* —6F **31**
Chapel La. *Bred* —7A **16**
Chapel La. *Hem* —5A **16**
Chapel La. *Up H'ling* —5A **12**
Chapel Rd. *Snod* —2C **22**
Chapel Rd. *Sut V* —6K **43**
Chapel St. *E Mal* —5H **27**
Chaplin Clo. *Wain* —4A **4**
Chapman Av. *Maid* —3D **36**
Chapman Way. *E Mal* —3G **27**
Chappell Way. *Sit* —3C **20**
Chapter Rd. *Roch* —1H **7**
Chard Ct. *Gill* —3G **9**
Chard Ho. *Maid* —4J **29**
Charing Rd. *Gill* —5B **10**
Chariot Way. *Roch* —5G **7**
Charlbury Clo. *Maid* —1F **35**
Charlecote Ct. Gill —1D 16 (off Derwent Way)
Charles Busby Ct. *Roy B* —2C **28**
Charles Clo. *Snod* —2C **22**
Charles Dickens Av. *High* —5E **2**
Charles Dri. *Cux* —5D **6**
Charles St. *Chat* —5C **8**
Charles St. *Maid* —1H **35**
Charles St. *Roch* —1J **7**
Charleworth Ho. *Chat* —6C **8**
Charlotte Clo. *Chat* —3F **15**
Charlotte Dri. *Gill* —7C **10**
Charlotte St. *Sit* —4C **20**
Charlton La. *W Far* —5A **34**
Charlton Mnr. *Gill* —3G **9**
Charlton St. *Maid* —2F **35**
Charter St. *Chat* —6D **8**
Charter St. *Gill* —1G **9**
Chart Hill Rd. *Cha S* —7E **42**
Chart Pl. *Gill* —6C **16**
Chart Rd. *Cha S* —6G **43**
Chart Sutton Bus. Est. *Cha S* —3G **43**
Chartway St. *Sut V* —4K **43**
Chartwell Clo. *Roch* —6K **3**
Chartwell Ct. *Gill* —3H **9**
Chartwell Gro. *Sit* —6A **20**
Chase, The. *Chat* —6B **8**
Chase, The. *Gill* —6A **10**
Chatham Gro. *Chat* —7D **8**
Chatham Hill. *Chat* —5F **9**
Chatham Rd. *Roch* —1B **24**
Chatsworth Dri. *Roch* —6K **3**
Chatsworth Dri. *Sit* —4K **19**
Chatsworth Rd. *Gill* —2G **9**
Chattenden Ct. *Maid* —4A **30**
Chattenden La. *Chatt* —3D **4**
Chattenden Ter. *Chatt* —3D **4**
Chaucer Clo. *Maid* —5D **36**
Chaucer Clo. *Roch* —1C **8**
Chaucer Rd. *Gill* —5H **9**
Chaucer Rd. *Sit* —6B **20**
Chaucer Way. *Lark* —7B **22**
Chegwell Dri. *Chat* —5F **15**
Chegworth Mill Cotts. *H'shm* —6H **39**
Chegworth Rd. *H'shm* —5G **39**
Chelmar Rd. *Chat* —4F **9**
Chelmsford Ho. *Maid* —6D **36**
Chelmsford Rd. *Roch* —2F **7**
Chelsfield Ho. *Maid* —6G **29**
Cheltenham Clo. *Maid* —6E **36**
Cheney Clo. *Gill* —4D **16**
Chepstow Ho. *Maid* —6E **36**
Chequers Clo. *Chat* —2E **24**
Chequers Ct. *Roch* —6J **3**
Chequers Shop. Cen. *Maid* —7K **29**
Cherbourg Cres. *Chat* —2D **14**
Cheriton Rd. *Gill* —2D **16**
Cheriton Way. *Maid* —4F **29** (in two parts)
Cherries, The. *Maid* —2C **34**
Cherry Amber Clo. *Gill* —1F **17**
Cherry Clo. *Sit* —3B **20**
Cherry Fields. *Sit* —4J **19**
Cherry Hill Ct. *N'tn* —3D **18**
Cherry Orchard. *Dit* —3K **27**
Cherry Orchard Way. *Maid* —1E **34**
Cherry Tree Rd. *Gill* —1F **17**
Cherry View. *Bou M* —2A **42**
Chervilles. *Maid* —2D **34**
Chesham Dri. *Gill* —3E **16**
Cheshire Rd. *Maid* —5D **36** (Westmorland Rd.)
Cheshire Rd. *Maid* —1D **36** (Willington St.)
Chester Clo. *Roch* —2F **7**
Chesterton Rd. *Lark* —6B **22**
Chestfield Clo. *Gill* —6E **10**
Chestnut Av. *Chat* —6C **14**
Chestnut Clo. *King H* —2B **32**
Chestnut Dri. *Cox* —2E **40**
Chestnut Ho. Barm —1D 34 (off Springwood Rd.)
Chestnut Rd. *Roch* —2G **7**
Chestnut St. *B'den* —5G **19**
Chestnut Wlk. *Lark* —1J **27**
Chestnut Wood La. *B'den* —6G **19**
Chetney Clo. *Roch* —1E **6**
Chevening Clo. *Chat* —4E **14**
Cheviot Gdns. *Down* —3F **37**
Cheyne Clo. *Kem* —1D **20**
Chicago Av. *Gill* —3K **9**
Chichester Clo. *Gill* —1G **17**
Chichester Ho. *Maid* —5C **36**
Chickfield Gdns. *Chat* —6G **9**
Chiddingstone Clo. *Maid* —6E **36**
Chieftain Clo. *Gill B* —7B **10**
Childscroft Rd. *Gill* —6F **11**
Chilham Clo. *Chat* —5C **8**
Chilham Rd. *Gill* —5A **10**
Chilham Rd. *Maid* —4F **29**
Chillington Clo. *Up H'lng* —5A **12**
Chillington St. *Maid* —5J **29**
Chillwack Rd. *Chatt* —2D **4**
Chiltern Clo. *Down* —3E **36**
Chilton Av. *Sit* —6D **20**
Chilton Ct. *Gill* —7E **10**
Chilton Dri. *High* —4D **2**
Chimes, The. *Roch* —3A **8**
Chippendale Clo. *Chat* —1D **24**
Chipstead Clo. *Maid* —5G **29**
Chipstead Rd. *Gill* —5D **16**
Chislehurst Clo. *Maid* —6E **36**
Chislet Wlk. *Gill* —5D **16**
Christchurch Ct. *Chat* —6G **9**
Christchurch Ho. *Maid* —7D **36**
Christen Way. *Maid* —2E **42**
Christie Clo. *Chat* —3F **15**
Christie Dri. *Lark* —6B **22**
Christmas St. *Gill* —1J **9**
Church Farm Clo. *Hoo* —3J **5**
Church Field. *Snod* —1D **22**
Church Fields. *W Mal* —3C **26**
Churchfields Ter. *Roch* —4K **7**
Church Grn. *Roch* —7A **4**
Church Hill. *Bap* —5J **21**
Church Hill. *Bou M* —3A **42**
Church Hill. *Chat* —6G **9**
Churchill Av. *Chat* —3D **14**
Churchill Cotts. *Leeds* —7A **38**
Churchill Ho. *Maid* —2E **34**
Churchill Ho. *Sit* —4F **21**
Churchill Sq. *King H* —1B **32**
Churchlands. *Chat* —7D **8**
Church La. *Barm* —3B **34**
Church La. *Bear* —7H **31**
Church La. *Chat* —2D **8**
Church La. *N'tn* —3D **18**
Church La. *W Far* —5A **34**
Church M. *Rain* —1F **17**
Church Path. *Gill* —2H **9** (Parr Av.)
Church Path. *Gill* —2F **9** (Prince Arthur Rd.)
Church Path. *Strood* —1K **7**
Church Pl. *Woul* —4E **12**
Church Rd. *Cha S* —5H **43**
Church Rd. *Murs* —5F **21**
Church Rd. *Rya* —1A **26**
Church Rd. *Tonge* —5J **21**
Church Rd. *Tovil* —2H **35**
Church Rd. Bus. Cen. *Sit* —3F **21**
Church Row. *Snod* —3C **22**
Church St. *Bou M* —2A **42**
Church St. *Burh* —2G **23**
Church St. *Chat* —4E **8** (in two parts)
Church St. *Gill* —2J **9**
Church St. *High* —1E **2**
Church St. *Hoo* —3J **5**
Church St. *Loose* —7J **35**
Church St. *Maid* —7K **29**
Church St. *Mil R* —4C **20**
Church St. *Roch* —4B **8**
Church St. *Sit* —5C **20**
Church St. *Tstn* —5H **33**
Church St. *Tovil* —2H **35**
Church Ter. *Chat* —6G **9**
Church Ter. *Maid* —1A **36**
Church Wlk. *Ayle* —7H **23**
Church Wlk. *E Mal* —4H **27**
Chute Clo. *Gill* —5D **16**
Cinnabar Clo. *Chat* —1E **24**
City Way. *Roch* —4B **8**
Claire Ho. *Maid* —6H **29**
Clandon Rd. *Chat* —7H **15**
Clare La. *E Mal* —3F **27**
Claremont Pl. *Chat* —5E **8**
Claremont Rd. *Maid* —6A **30**
Claremont Way. *Chat* —5D **8**
Clarence Av. *Roch* —4A **8**
Clarence Ct. *Weav* —7D **30**
Clarence Rd. *Chat* —6F **9**
Clarendon Clo. *Bear* —7F **31**
Clarendon Gdns. *Roch* —6J **3**
Clarendon Pl. Maid —7K 29 (off King St.)
Clare Wood Dri. *E Mal* —3F **27**
Clark M. *Roy B* —2C **28**
Clavell Clo. *Gill* —6E **16**
Claygate. *Maid* —3C **36**
Cleave Rd. *Gill* —6J **9**
Clematis Av. *Gill* —4B **16**
Clement Ct. *Maid* —6G **29**
Clerke Dri. *Kem* —1E **20**
Clermont Clo. *Hem* —6A **16**
Cleveland Ho. *Maid* —2E **34**
Cleveland Rd. *Gill* —2H **9**
Clewson Rise. *Maid* —3A **30**
Cliffe Rd. *Strood* —5J **3**
Cliff Hill. *Bou M* —1B **42**
Cliff Hill Rd. *Langl* —1B **42**
Clifton Clo. *Maid* —6A **30**
Clifton Clo. *Roch* —2H **7**
Clifton Rd. *Gill* —1G **9**

46 A-Z Maidstone, Chatham, Gillingham & Rochester

Earl Clo.—Globe La.

Earl Clo. *Chat* —5F **15**
Earl St. *Maid* —7J **29**
East Ct. *Maid* —3K **35**
East Ct. Cotts. *Det* —2F **31**
Eastcourt Cres. *Gill* —5B **10**
Eastcourt La. *Gill* —4B **10**
(in three parts)
Eastern Rd. *Gill* —2K **9**
Eastfield Ho. *Maid* —2E **34**
Eastfields. *E Mal* —6J **27**
East Ga. *Roch* —3A **8**
Eastgate Ct. *Roch* —3A **8**
Eastgate Ter. *Roch* —3A **8**
East Grn. *Kem* —1E **20**
E. Hall Hill. *Bou M* —7D **42**
E. Hall La. *Sit* —4G **21**
East Hill. *Chat* —7H **9**
Eastling Clo. *Gill* —5D **10**
E. Park Rd. *Roy B* —2D **28**
East Row. *Roch* —3A **8**
Eastry Clo. *Maid* —4F **29**
East St. *Chat* —5E **8**
East St. *Gill* —2H **9**
East St. *Hunt* —7C **40**
East St. *Sit* —5E **20**
East St. *Snod* —2D **22**
Eastwell Clo. *Maid* —6B **30**
Eastwood Rd. *Sit* —4B **20**
Ebony Wlk. *Maid* —1E **34**
Eccles Row. *Eccl* —4H **23**
Eccleston Rd. *Tovil* —2J **35**
Echo Clo. *Maid* —6E **36**
Echo Ho. *Sit* —6F **21**
Eddington Clo. *Maid* —6A **36**
Eden Av. *Chat* —2D **14**
Edgar Pl. *Maid* —7K **29**
Edgeler Ct. *Snod* —3A **22**
Edinburgh Rd. *Chat* —6G **9**
Edinburgh Rd. *Gill* —3H **9**
Edinburgh Sq. *Maid* —6B **36**
Edisbury Wlk. *Gill* —4D **16**
Edmund Clo. *Barm* —1D **34**
Edna Rd. *Maid* —4J **29**
Edward Ct. *Chat* —7G **9**
Edwards Clo. *Gill* —4C **16**
Edward St. *Chat* —5E **8**
Edward St. *Roch* —1K **7**
Edward Wlk. *E Mal* —3G **27**
Edwin Rd. *Gill* —1B **16**
Edyngham Clo. *Kem* —1E **20**
Egerton Rd. *Maid* —4H **29**
Egremont Rd. *Bear* —2E **36**
Egypt Pl. *Bear* —7H **31**
Elaine Av. *Roch* —1G **7**
Elaine Ct. *Roch* —2G **7**
Elder Ct. *Gill* —3B **16**
Eldon St. *Chat* —4E **8**
Elgin Gdns. *Roch* —3F **7**
Elham Clo. *Gill* —6B **10**
Eling Ct. *Maid* —4K **35**
Elizabeth Clo. *Maid* —7K **29**
Elizabeth Ct. *Gill* —7C **10**
Elizabeth Ho. *Maid* —5K **29**
Elizabeth Smith Ct. *E Mal* —4G **27**
Ellenswood Clo. *Down* —3E **36**
Ellingham Leas. *Maid* —5B **36**
Ellison Way. *Gill* —6G **11**
Elm Av. *Chat* —7C **8**
Elm Av. *Chatt* —3E **4**
(in two parts)
Elm Clo. *High* —4E **2**
Elm Ct. Ind. Est. *Hem* —6J **15**
Elm Cres. *E Mal* —3G **27**
Elmfield. *Gill* —5A **10**
Elmfield Ct. *Cox* —2F **41**
Elm Gro. *Maid* —1A **36**
Elm Gro. *Sit* —5F **21**
Elmhurst Gdns. *Chat* —5B **8**
Elm Rd. *Gill* —2J **9**
Elmscroft Farm Cotts. *Maid* —6B **34**
Elmstone Clo. *Maid* —2E **34**
Elmstone La. *Maid* —2E **34**
Elmstone Rd. *Gill* —2D **16**
Elm Tree Dri. *Roch* —6J **7**
Elm Vs. *Chatt* —2D **4**
Elm Wlk. *Ayle* —2B **28**
Elmwood Rd. *Chatt* —1D **4**
Elphinstone Ho. *Maid* —4J **29**
Elvington Clo. *Maid* —6G **29**
Ely Clo. *Gill* —6E **10**
Ely Ho. *Maid* —5C **36**
Embassy Clo. *Gill* —7K **9**
Emerald Clo. *Roch* —2B **14**
Emily Rd. *Chat* —3F **15**
Emsworth Gro. *Maid* —5C **30**
Englefield Cres. *Cli* —1K **3**
Ennerdale Ho. *Maid* —5D **36**
Enterprise Bus. Est. *Roch* —1C **8**
Enterprise Cen., The. *Chat* —2G **25**
Enterprise Clo. *Roch* —7B **4**
Enterprise Rd. *Maid* —3K **35**
Epaul La. *Roch* —2A **8**
Epps Rd. *Sit* —6C **20**
Epsom Clo. *Maid* —6E **36**
Epsom Clo. *W Mal* —3B **26**
Erith Clo. *Maid* —3K **29**
Ernest Rd. *Chat* —5E **8**
Esplanade. *Roch* —5J **7**
Esplanade. *Strood* —2K **7**
Essex Rd. *Hall* —4C **12**
Essex Rd. *Maid* —6D **36**
Estelle Clo. *Roch* —2B **14**
Esther Ct. *Mil R* —1C **20**
Ethelbert Rd. *Roch* —4A **8**
Ethel-Maud Ct. *Gill* —1H **9**
Eton Clo. *Chat* —5D **14**
Eurolink Commercial Pk. *Sit* —4E **20**
Eurolink Ind. Est. *Sit* —5F **21**
Eurolink Way. *Sit* —5D **20**
Eva Rd. *Gill* —5H **9**
Evelyn Rd. *Maid* —1H **35**
Everest Dri. *Hoo* —3J **5**
Everest La. *Roch* —6K **3**
Everest M. *Hoo* —3J **5**
Everglades, The. *Hem* —3K **15**
Evergreen Clo. *Hem* —4A **16**
Evergreen Clo. *High* —4D **2**
Evergreen Clo. *Leyb* —1F **27**
Eversley Clo. *Maid* —5F **29**
Ewart Rd. *Chat* —7C **8**
Ewell Av. *W Mal* —3B **26**
Ewell La. *W Far* —7K **33**
Exeter Ho. *Maid* —5C **36**
Exeter Wlk. *Roch* —2A **14**
Exmouth Rd. *Gill* —1G **9**
Exton Clo. *Chat* —7G **15**
Exton Gdns. *Weav* —5E **30**
Eyhorne St. *Holl* —3C **38**
Eynsford Rd. *Maid* —4G **29**

Factory Cotts. *Cux* —5F **7**
Factory Cotts. *Woul* —5E **12**
Fagus Clo. *Chat* —1F **25**
Fairbourne La. *H'sme* —7K **39**
Fairfax Bus. Cen. *Maid* —1E **42**
Fairfax Clo. *Gill* —4D **16**
Fairfax Ho. *Maid* —7D **36**
Fairhurst Dri. *E Far* —1E **40**
Fairlawn Clo. *Tstn* —4H **33**
Fairlead Rd. *Roch* —7B **8**
Fairleas. *Sit* —7F **21**
Fairmeadow. *Maid* —7J **29**
Fairservice Clo. *Sit* —4G **21**
Fairview Av. *Gill* —4B **16**
Fairview Cotts. *Loose* —7J **35**
Fairview Cotts. *W Far* —6B **34**
Fairview Dri. *High* —3D **2**
Fairview Rd. *Sit* —6E **20**
Fairway Clo. *Roch* —7A **8**
Fairway, The. *Roch* —7A **8**
Fairway, The. *Sit* —7C **20**
Falcon Ct. *Sit* —7E **20**
Falcon Grn. *Lark* —2G **27**
Falkland Pl. *Chat* —1C **24**
Fallowfield. *Chat* —1F **15**
Fallowfield. *Sit* —7E **20**
Fallowfield Clo. *Weav* —7D **30**
Fanconi Rd. *Chat* —6F **15**
Fancy Row. *Bear* —6H **31**
Fane Way. *Gill* —5C **16**
(in two parts)
Fant La. *Maid* —2E **34**
Faraday Rd. *Maid* —4B **30**
Fareham Wlk. *Maid* —6E **36**
Farleigh Bri. *E Far* —4D **34**
Farleigh Ct. *Maid* —2D **34**
Farleigh Hill. *Tovil* —1H **35**
Farleigh Hill Retail Pk. *Tovil* —3H **35**
Farleigh La. *Maid* —2D **34**
Farleigh Trad. Est. *Tovil* —3H **35**
Farley Clo. *Chat* —7H **15**
Farm Cotts. *Maid* —3C **36**
Farm Cres. *Sit* —7E **20**
Farmdale Av. *Roch* —6H **7**
Farmer Clo. *Leeds* —6B **38**
Farm Hill Av. *Roch* —6H **3**
Farm Rd. *Chat* —6C **14**
Farnborough Clo. *Maid* —2F **35**
Farne Clo. *Maid* —6K **35**
Farnham Clo. *Rain* —7H **11**
Farningham Clo. *Maid* —5B **30**
Farraday Clo. *Roch* —1B **14**
Farrier Clo. *Weav* —6D **30**
Fartherwell Av. *W Mal* —3B **26**
Fartherwell Rd. *W Mal* —4A **26**
Farthings Cotts. *S'lng* —2J **29**
Fathom Ho. *Roch* —7A **8**
Fauchon's Clo. *Bear* —1E **36**
Fauchon's La. *Bear* —1E **36**
Fawley Clo. *Maid* —4H **29**
Featherby Rd. *Gill* —6A **10**
(in two parts)
Featherbys Cotts. *Gill* —2K **9**
Felderland Clo. *Maid* —7C **36**
Felderland Dri. *Maid* —7D **36**
Felderland Rd. *Maid* —7D **36**
Fellows Clo. *Gill* —4B **16**
Fernbank Clo. *Chat* —7C **14**
Ferndale Rd. *Gill* —3J **9**
Ferndown Clo. *Hem* —4A **16**
Fernhill Rd. *Maid* —2D **34**
Fernleigh. *Sit* —7B **20**
Fernleigh Rise. *Dit* —1J **27**
Fernleigh Ter. *Sit* —7B **20**
Ferns, The. *Lark* —2J **27**
Fern Wlk. *Sit* —4G **21**
Ferrier Clo. *Gill* —5E **16**
Ferry La. *Woul* —5E **12**
Ferry Rd. *Hall* —5C **12**
Ffinch Clo. *Dit* —3A **28**
Field Clo. *Chat* —3C **14**
Fielder Clo. *Sit* —4G **21**
Field Ga. *Sit* —7C **20**
Fielding Dri. *Lark* —7C **22**
Fieldings, The. *Sit* —7C **20**
Fields La. *W'bury* —5F **33**
Fieldspar Clo. *Chat* —1D **24**
Fieldworks Rd. *Gill* —1E **8**
Fiji Ter. *Maid* —4K **29**
Finch Ct. *Maid* —4H **29**
Finches, The. *Sit* —6D **20**
Findlay Clo. *Gill* —4D **16**
Findley Ho. *Maid* —4J **29**
Finglesham Ct. *Maid* —4B **36**
Fintonagh Dri. *Maid* —4A **30**
Finwell Rd. *Gill* —6G **11**
Firethorn Clo. *Gill* —2K **9**
Firs Clo. *Ayle* —2B **28**
Firs La. *Holl* —2K **37**
First Av. *Chat* —6G **9**
First Av. *Gill* —6J **9**
Fir Tree Gro. *Chat* —1H **25**
Fisher Rd. *Chat* —2F **15**
Fisher St. *Maid* —5K **29**
Fitzwilliam Rd. *Bear* —6E **30**
Five Bells La. *Roch* —4B **8**
Fiveways Ct. *Chat* —4E **8**
Flack Gdns. *Hoo* —2J **5**
Flamingo Clo. *Chat* —2E **14**
Flaxman Dri. *Maid* —5F **29**
Flaxmans Ct. *Bromp* —2E **8**
Fleet Rd. *Roch* —7B **8**
Flint Grn. *Chat* —7G **15**
Flood Hatch. *Maid* —2G **35**
Florence Rd. *Maid* —1H **35**
Florence St. *Roch* —7K **3**
Flower Rise. *Maid* —5J **29**
Flume End. *Maid* —2G **35**
Foley St. *Maid* —6K **29**
*Folkestone Ho. Maid —6E **36***
(off Fontwell Clo.)
Fontwell Clo. *Maid* —6E **36**
Foord Almshouses. *Roch* —5K **7**
Foord St. *Roch* —4A **8**
Fordcombe Clo. *Maid* —5E **36**
Fordingbridge Clo. *Maid* —6E **28**
Fordwich Clo. *Maid* —4E **28**
Fordwich Grn. *Gill* —5C **10**
Foremans Barn Rd. *Maid* —2C **40**
Forestdale Rd. *Chat* —2E **24**
Forest Dri. *Chat* —7D **14**
Foresters Clo. *Chat* —7D **14**
Forest Hill. *Maid* —3J **35**
Forest Way. *King H* —1B **32**
Forge Bungalows. *Maid* —3C **36**
*Forge Cotts. Bear —7H **31***
(off Green, The)
Forge Cotts. *Langl* —2A **42**
Forge La. *Boxl* —7G **25**
Forge La. *Bred* —7K **15**
Forge La. *Cha S* —7E **42**
Forge La. *E Far* —5E **34**
Forge La. *Gill* —2J **9**
Forge La. *High* —5E **2**
Forge La. *Leeds* —5K **37**
Forge La. *Shorne* —4A **2**
Forge Meadow. *H'shm* —6K **39**
Forge Rd. *Sit* —3C **20**
Formby Rd. *Hall* —3C **12**
Formby Ter. *Hall* —3C **12**
Forsham La. *Cha S* —7J **43**
Forstal Cotts. *Ayle* —1E **28**
Forstal La. *Cox* —1G **41**
Forstal Rd. *Ayle* —1D **28**
Forsters. *Langl* —1K **43**
Forsyth Clo. *E Mal* —2H **27**
Forsyth Ct. *Gill* —1G **9**
Fort Bridgewood. *Roch* —2K **13**
Fort Pitt Hill. *Chat* —4C **8**
Fort Pitt St. *Chat* —5C **8**
Fort St. *Roch* —4B **8**
Forum, The. *Sit* —5D **20**
Foster Clark Est. *Maid* —2A **36**
Foster St. *Maid* —1K **35**
Fostington Way. *Chat* —1C **24**
Foulds Clo. *Gill* —4B **16**
Fountain Enterprise Pk. *Maid* —3K **35**
Fountain La. *Maid* —2D **34**
Fountain Rd. *Roch* —6G **3**
Fountain St. *Sit* —5C **20**
Four Acres. *E Mal* —6J **27**
Four Elms Hill. *Chatt* —3D **4**
Fourth Av. *Gill* —4J **9**
Fourwents Rd. *Hoo* —1H **5**
Fowey Clo. *Chat* —4G **15**
Fowler Clo. *Gill* —6C **16**
Foxburrow Clo. *Gill* —4D **16**
Foxden Dri. *Down* —3E **36**
Foxglove Cres. *Chat* —5C **14**
Foxglove Rise. *Maid* —4H **29**
Foxgrove. *Mil R* —2C **20**
Foxgrove Row. *Hall* —4B **12**
Fox Hill. *Bap* —6H **21**
Fox St. *Gill* —2G **9**
Foxtail Clo. *St Mi* —5F **5**
Frances Cotts. *Hoo* —1J **5**
Francis Dri. *Chat* —7E **14**
Francis Est. *Maid* —1F **43**
Francis La. *Maid* —7E **36**
Frank Apps Clo. *N'tn* —3D **18**
Franklin Dri. *Weav* —7C **30**
Franklin Rd. *Gill* —3H **9**
Franklins Cotts. *Maid* —7F **35**
Franks Ct. *Gill* —6B **10**
Frederick Rd. *Gill* —4G **9**
Frederick St. *Sit* —5C **20**
Freelands Rd. *Snod* —2B **22**
Freemans Gdns. *Chat* —6D **8**
Freeman Way. *Maid* —4D **36**
Freesia Clo. *Gill* —3K **9**
Fremlins Rd. *Bear* —7H **31**
Frensham Clo. *Sit* —5F **21**
Frensham Wlk. *Chat* —1D **24**
Freshland Rd. *Maid* —7E **28**
Freshwater Rd. *Chat* —2F **15**
Friars Av. *Chat* —7D **14**
Friars Ct. *Maid* —7K **29**
Friary Pl. *Roch* —1K **7**
Friary Precinct. *Roch* —1K **7**
Frindsbury Hill. *Roch* —6A **4**
Frindsbury Rd. *Strood* —7K **3**
Frinstead Wlk. *Maid* —4F **29**
Frinsted Clo. *Gill* —5C **10**
Friston Way. *Roch* —1B **14**
Frithwood Clo. *Down* —3E **36**
Frittenden Rd. *Wain* —5B **4**
Frobisher Ct. *Mil R* —3C **20**
Frobisher Gdns. *Roch* —6A **8**
Frog La. *W Mal* —3D **26**
Frost Cres. *Chat* —2E **14**
Froyle Clo. *Maid* —5F **29**
Fulbert Dri. *Bear* —6E **30**
Fullers Clo. *Bear* —7F **31**
Fulmar Rd. *Roch* —2F **7**
Fulston Pl. *Sit* —6E **20**
Furfield Clo. *Maid* —7D **36**
Furrells Rd. *Roch* —3B **8**

Gable Cotts. *Loose* —7J **35**
Gable Cotts. *Otham* —5G **37**
Gabriel's Hill. *Maid* —7K **29**
Gadby Rd. *Sit* —4A **20**
Gads Hill. *Gill* —1K **9**
Gads Hill Pl. *High* —5E **2**
Gagetown Ter. *Maid* —4J **29**
Gainsborough Clo. *Gill* —3D **16**
Gainsborough Clo. *Sit* —4K **19**
Gainsborough Dri. *Maid* —7E **28**
Galahad Av. *Roch* —2G **7**
Galbri Dri. *Roch* —2J **7**
Galena Clo. *Chat* —1E **24**
Gallants La. *E Far* —5C **34**
Galleon Clo. *Roch* —1A **14**
Gandy's La. *Bou M* —3B **42**
Garden Clo. *Maid* —5D **36**
Gardenia Clo. *Roch* —5K **3**
Garden of England Mobile Home Pk., The. *H'shm* —5J **39**
Gardens, The. *Cox* —2F **41**
(in two parts)
Garden St. *Gill* —2E **8**
Garden Way. *King H* —2B **32**
Gardiner St. *Gill* —2G **9**
Garfield Rd. *Gill* —2H **9**
Garrington Clo. *Maid* —5B **30**
Gas Ho. Rd. *Roch* —2A **8**
Gas Rd. *Murs* —3F **21**
Gas Rd. *Sit* —4D **20**
Gassons Rd. *Snod* —2A **22**
Gatcombe Clo. *Chat* —4E **14**
Gatcombe Clo. *Maid* —6E **28**
Gatland La. *Maid* —3D **34**
Gault Clo. *Bear* —2F **37**
Gayhurst Clo. *Gill* —3D **16**
Gayhurst Dri. *Sit* —4A **20**
Gaze Hill Av. *Sit* —6E **20**
Gean Clo. *Chat* —1E **24**
Genesta Clo. *Sit* —2C **20**
Geneva Av. *Gill* —6A **10**
Gentian Clo. *Chat* —5C **14**
(in two parts)
Gentian Clo. *Weav* —6D **30**
George La. *Leeds* —5B **38**
George La. *Roch* —2A **8**
George Marsham Ho. *Maid* —2J **41**
George St. *Hunt* —7D **40**
George St. *Maid* —1K **35**
George St. *Sit* —6F **21**
George Summers Clo. *Roch* —7C **4**
Georgian Dri. *Cox* —2G **41**
Georgian Way. *Gill* —5C **16**
Gerald Av. *Chat* —6D **8**
Gerrard Av. *Roch* —1B **14**
Gerrards Dri. *Sit* —7D **20**
Gibbons Rd. *Sit* —4K **19**
Gibbs Hill. *Nett* —7C **32**
Gibraltar Av. *Gill* —1E **8**
Gibraltar Hill. *Chat* —4D **8**
Gibraltar La. *Maid* —3H **29**
Gibson Dri. *King H* —7A **26**
Gibson St. *Sit* —5C **20**
Gidds Pond Cotts. *Weav* —5D **30**
Giddyhorn La. *Maid* —7F **29**
Gifford Clo. *Gill* —5C **10**
Gigghill Rd. *Lark* —7B **22**
Gilbert Clo. *Hem* —4A **16**
Gilbert Ter. *Maid* —4K **29**
*Giles Young Ct. Mil R —4C **20***
(off St Paul's St.)
Gill Av. *Wain* —4B **4**
Gilletts La. *E Mal* —5H **27**
Gillingham Bus. Cen. *Gill* —7K **9**
Gillingham Bus. Pk. *Gill* —7A **10**
Gillingham Ga. Rd. *Gill* —1G **9**
Gillingham Grn. *Gill* —2J **9**
Gillingham Northern Link Rd. *Chat* —7F **5**
Gillingham Rd. *Gill* —4G **9**
Gill's Cotts. *Roch* —3C **8**
Gills Ct. *Roch* —1C **8**
Ginsbury Clo. *Roch* —2C **8**
Ginsbury Ho. *Roch* —2B **8**
Glade, The. *Chat* —7E **14**
Gladstone Rd. *Chat* —6C **8**
Gladstone Rd. *Maid* —5K **29**
Gladwyn Clo. *Gill* —5D **16**
(in two parts)
Glamford Rd. *Roch* —3F **7**
Glamis Clo. *Chat* —4E **14**
Glanville Rd. *Gill* —3H **9**
Glanville Rd. *Roch* —1J **7**
Glasgow Ho. *Maid* —5D **36**
Gleaming Wood Dri. *Chat* —2G **25**
Gleaners Clo. *Weav* —7D **30**
Gleanings M. *Roch* —3A **8**
Glebe La. *Maid* —3C **34**
Glebe La. *Sit* —7F **21**
Glebe Meadow. *W'bury* —5F **33**
Glebe Rd. *Gill* —5J **9**
Glebe, The. *Cux* —6E **6**
Glenbrook Gro. *Sit* —2C **20**
Glencoe Rd. *Chat* —6E **8**
Gleneagles Ct. *Chat* —7D **14**
Gleneagles Dri. *Maid* —3J **35**
Glenwood Clo. *Chat* —7G **9**
Glenwood Clo. *Hem* —3A **16**
Glenwood Clo. *Maid* —6F **29**
Glistening Glade. *Gill* —3E **16**
Globe La. *Chat* —4D **8**
(in two parts)

48 A-Z Maidstone, Chatham, Gillingham & Rochester

Gloucester Clo.—Hoath Clo.

Gloucester Clo. Gill —1G 17
Gloucester Rd. Maid —4C 36
Glovers Cres. Sit —6D 20
Glovers Mill. Roch —5B 8
Glynne Clo. Gill —3D 16
Godden Rd. Snod —2B 22
Goddings Dri. Roch —5J 7
Goddington La. H'shm —6J 39
Goddington Rd. Roch —7K 3
Godfrey Clo. Roch —6H 3
Godlands, The. Tovil —3J 35
Golden Wood Clo. Chat —2H 25
Goldfinch Clo. Lark —1H 27
Golding Clo. Dit —2K 27
Goldings Clo. King H —2B 32
Goldings, The. Gill —1C 16
Goldsmith Rd. Gill —4E 16
Goldstone Wlk. Chat —1E 24
Goldsworth Dri. Roch —6J 3
Goldthorne Clo. Maid —7B 30
Goodall Clo. Gill —4E 16
Goodnestone Rd. Sit —6F 21
Goodwin Dri. Maid —3A 30
Goodwood Clo. Maid —6E 36
Goose Clo. Chat —2E 14
Gordon Clo. Sit —5G 21
Gordon Ct. Maid —2H 41
Gordon Rd. Chat —6E 8
(Magpie Hall Rd.)
Gordon Rd. Chat —1E 8
(South Rd.)
Gordon Rd. Gill —3J 9
Gordon Rd. Hoo —2H 5
Gordon Rd. Roch —1J 7
Gordon Ter. Roch —4A 8
Gore Ct. Rd. Otham —7E 36
Gore Ct. Rd. Sit —7C 20
Gore Grn. Rd. High —1F 3
Gorham Clo. Snod —3B 22
Gorham Dri. Down —3F 37
Gorse Av. Chat —5C 14
Gorse Cres. Dit —3A 28
Gorse Rd. Roch —7H 3
(in two parts)
Gorse Rd. Sit —4F 21
Gorst St. Gill —3G 9
Goudhurst Clo. Maid —7H 29
Goudhurst Rd. Gill —5B 10
Gould Rd. Chat —6F 15
Goulston. Maid —6B 34
Grace Av. Maid —5G 29
(in two parts)
Grafton Av. Roch —1C 14
Grafton Rd. Sit —5D 20
Grafton Way. Sit —5E 20
Graham Clo. Gill —2D 8
Grainey Field. H'lip —5A 18
Grain Rd. Gill —5B 16
Grampian Way. Down —3F 37
Granada St. Maid —7K 29
Granary Clo. Gill —7F 11
Granary Clo. Weav —6D 30
Grandsire Gdns. Hoo —1J 5
Grange Clo. Leyb —1D 26
Grange Cotts. Maid —6H 37
Grange Hill. Chat —5F 9
Grange Ho. Maid —2D 34
Grange La. S'lng —1J 29
(in two parts)
Grange Rd. Gill —2J 9
Grange Rd. Roch —1K 7
Grange, The. E Mal —4H 27
Grange Way. Roch —5A 8
Grant Clo. Gill B —7B 10
Grant Rd. Wain —4A 4
Granville Ct. Maid —5K 29
Granville Rd. Gill —3J 9
Granville Rd. Maid —5K 29
Grapple Rd. Maid —4J 29
Grasmere Gro. Roch —6A 4
Grasslands. Langl —1K 43
Grassmere. Leyb —2G 27
Grassy Glade. Hem —3B 16
Gravelly Bottom Rd. Kgswd —2K 43
Gravel Wlk. Roch —3B 8
Graveney Clo. Cli —1A 4
Graveney Rd. Maid —5E 36
Gravesend Rd. High —5F 3
Gravesend Rd. Shorne —3A 2
Grayshott Clo. Sit —6D 20
Gt. Ivy Mill Cotts. Maid —5J 35
Great Lines. Gill —3E 8
Gt. South Av. Chat —7E 8
Grebe Ct. Lark —2G 27
Grecian St. Maid —5K 29
Green Acre Clo. Chat —4E 14
Greenbank. Chat —1F 15
Green Bank Clo. Hem —4A 16
Greenborough Clo. Maid —6D 36
Green Clo. Roch —6B 8
Green Farm La. Shorne —1A 2
Greenfield Clo. Eccl —4J 23
Greenfield Cotts. Boxl —7G 25
Greenfield Rd. Gill —2J 9
Greenfields. Maid —4D 36
Greenfields Clo. Wain —4B 4
Greenfinches. Hem —3K 15
Green Hill. Otham —4G 37
Greenhill Cotts. Maid —4G 37
Greenhithe. Maid —1J 35
Green La. Bou M —2A 42
Green La. Langl —2K 43
Green La. Shorne —5A 2
Green La. Cotts. Langl —2K 43
Green Porch Clo. Sit —2D 20
Greensands. W'slde —2G 25
Green's Cotts. Maid —1D 40
Greenside. Maid —1A 36
Green St. Gill —3G 9
Green, The. Bear —7H 31
Green, The. Bou M —2A 42
Green, The. E Far —5E 34
Green, The. W Mal —3D 26
Greenvale Gdns. Gill —6B 10
Greenview Wlk. Gill —4A 10
Greenway. Chat —4B 14
Green Way. Maid —1E 34
Greenway Ct. Rd. Holl —2F 39
Greenway La. H'shm —5G 39
Greenways. Sit —6F 21
Greenways. Weav —6E 30
Greenwich Clo. Chat —5G 15
Greenwich Clo. Maid —7G 29
Gregory Clo. Gill —5E 16
Gregory Clo. Kem —1E 20
Grenadier Clo. Rain —6H 11
Gresham Clo. Rain —7F 11
Gresham Rd. Cox —2G 41
Greyfriars. Maid —6G 29
Greystones Rd. Bear —2F 37
Grey Wethers. S'lng —6C 24
Grizedale Clo. Roch —1B 14
Groombridge Sq. Maid —6E 36
Grosvenor Av. Chat —5C 8
Grosvenor Ho. Maid —7E 36
Grosvenor Rd. Gill B —7K 9
Grove Grn. La. Weav —6D 30
Grove Grn. Rd. Weav —6E 30
Grovehurst Av. Kem —1D 20
Grove La. Hunt —5A 40
Grove Pk. Av. Sit —4K 19
Grove Rd. Chat —6F 9
Grove Rd. Gill —2A 10
Grove Rd. Maid —6B 36
Grove Rd. Roch —7K 3
Grove Rd. Up H'lng —4A 12
Groves, The. Snod —3B 22
Grove, The. Bear —1F 37
Grovewood Ct. Weav —7D 30
Grovewood Dri. Weav —7C 30
Guardian Ct. Gill —7C 10
Guildford Gdns. Roch —2E 6
Guildford Ho. Maid —5C 36
Gullands. Langl —1K 43
Gundulph Ho. Roch —2A 8
Gundulph Rd. Chat —4C 8
Gundulph Sq. Roch —2A 8
Gun La. Strood —1J 7
Gunnis Clo. Gill —5D 16
Guston Rd. Maid —6B 30

Hacket Ho. Maid —4K 29
Hackney Rd. Maid —2F 35
Hadleigh Ct. Hem —6A 16
Hadley Gdns. Holl —2F 39
Hadlow Rd. Maid —6B 30
Haig Av. Chat —6E 8
Haig Av. Gill —4J 9
Haig Av. Roch —7B 8
Haig Vs. Chatt —2E 4
Halden Clo. Maid —6E 36
Hale Rd. Cli —1A 4
Haleys Pl. Burh —2J 23
Halfpenny Clo. Maid —2D 34
Half Yoke. Maid —4E 34
Halifax Clo. Chat —3F 15
Hall Clo. Sit —3C 20
Halling By-Pass. Hall —3C 12
Halling Farm Cotts. Up H'lng —4A 12
Hall Rd. Ayle —3B 28
Hall Rd. Chat —6G 15
Hall Rd. Woul —6E 12
Halls Cotts. Det —2F 31
Hallsfield Rd. Chat —6B 14
Hallwood Clo. Gill —4D 16
Hallwood Ho. Chat —7G 15
Halstead Wlk. Maid —4F 29
Halstow Clo. Maid —7A 36
Hambledon Ct. Maid —1E 34
Hambrook Wlk. Sit —1D 20
Hamelin Rd. Gill —1K 15
Hamilton Ct. Chat —7G 9
Hamilton Cres. Sit —6A 20
Hamilton Ho. Maid —7D 36
Hamilton Rd. Gill —1H 9
Ham La. Gill —6H 15
Hammond Hill. Chat —4C 8
Hammond's Sq. Snod —2C 22
Hampden Way. W Mal —1A 32
Hampshire Clo. Chat —2G 15
Hampshire Dri. Maid —4B 36
Hampson Way. Bear —7F 31
Hampton Clo. Chat —4E 14
Hampton Rd. Maid —5B 30
Ham River Hill. Cli —1J 3
Hamwick Grn. Chat —1G 25
Hanbury Clo. W'bury —5F 33
Hancock Clo. Roch —6K 3
Hanover Clo. Sit —7C 20
Hanover Ct. Maid —6A 30
Hanover Dri. Gill —5C 16
Hanover Grn. Lark —7A 22
Hanover Rd. Cox —2F 41
Hanway. Gill —6A 10
Harbledown Mnr. Gill —5B 10
(off Goudhurst Rd.)
Harbourland Clo. Maid —3A 30
Harbourland Cotts. Maid —3B 30
Harbour, The. Sut V —7K 43
Harcourt Gdns. Gill —5E 16
Hardie Clo. E Mal —2G 27
Hardinge Clo. Gill —5D 16
Hards Town. Chat —4E 8
Hardwick Ho. Maid —4D 36
Hardy Clo. Chat —3F 15
Hardy St. Maid —5K 29
Harebell Clo. Chat —5C 14
Harebell Clo. Weav —6D 30
Haredale Clo. Roch —2B 14
Hare St. Chat —5F 9
Harkness Ct. Sit —5F 21
Harlech Clo. Strood —6H 3
Harold Av. Gill —4J 9
Harold Rd. Cux —5E 6
Harold Rd. Sit —6F 21
Harp Farm Rd. Boxl —3G 25
Harple La. Det —2E 30
Harptree Dri. Chat —4C 14
Harrier Dri. Sit —7E 20
Harris Gdns. Sit —4G 21
Harrisons Cres. Sit —3B 20
Harrow Cotts. Langl —1K 43
Harrow Ct. Chat —5G 15
Harrow Rd. Hem —3K 15
Harrow Way. Weav —6D 30
Hartington St. Chat —5E 8
Hartley Clo. Maid —6E 36
Hartlip Hill. H'lip —2A 18
Hartnup St. Maid —2F 35
Hartpiece Clo. Gill —6F 11
Hartridge Cvn. Pk. E Far —5D 34
Hart St. Maid —1J 35
Hart St. Commercial Cen. Maid —1J 35
Harty Av. Gill —6B 16
Harvel Av. Roch —1H 7
Harvesters Clo. Gill —3E 16
Harvesters Way. Weav —7C 30
Harvest Ridge. Leyb —1E 26
Harvey Dri. Sit —7E 20
Harvey Rd. Gill —1E 16
Harwood Rd. Gill —7H 11
Hasledon Cotts. High —1E 2
Haslemere Est. Maid —7E 36
Hasted Rd. N'tn —2D 18
Hasteds. Holl —2E 38
Haste Hill Clo. Bou M —2K 41
Haste Hill Rd. Bou M —2K 41
Hastings Rd. Maid —1A 36
Hatfield Rd. Roch —7J 3
Hathaway Ct. Gill —1D 16
Hathaway Ct. Roch —3K 7
Hatherall Rd. Maid —5A 30
Hatton Rd. Chat —6G 15
Havant Wlk. Maid —6E 36
Haven Clo. Roch —6A 8
Haven St. Wain —1K 3
Haven Way. St Mi —6F 5
Havisham Clo. Roch —6B 8
Havock La. Maid —7J 29
Hawbeck Rd. Gill —6C 16
Hawkes Rd. Eccl —5H 23
Hawkhurst Rd. Gill —5A 10
Hawkins Clo. Chat —2D 8
Hawkins Clo. Mil R —2C 20
Hawkwood. Maid —6E 28
Hawkwood Clo. Roch —4B 8
Hawley Ct. Maid —7H 29
Hawser Rd. Roch —7A 8
Hawthorne Av. Gill —7C 10
Hawthorn Ho. Barm —1D 34
(off Springwood Rd.)
Hawthorn Ho. Chat —4D 14
Hawthorn Rd. Roch —2F 7
Hawthorn Rd. Sit —5C 20
Hawthorns. Chat —1D 24
Hawthorns, The. Ayle —2B 28
Hayes Clo. High —4E 2
Hayes Ter. Shorne —4A 2
Hayfield. Leyb —1F 27
Hayfields. Chat —7H 15
Hayle Mill Cotts. Maid —4J 35
Hayle Mill Rd. Maid —3J 35
Hayle Rd. Maid —1K 35
Hayley Clo. Cux —6D 6
Hayman Wlk. Eccl —4H 23
Haymen St. Chat —5C 8
Hayrick Clo. Weav —6D 30
Haysel. Sit —7E 20
Hays Rd. Snod —4B 22
Haywain Clo. Weav —7E 30
Hayward Av. Roch —7K 3
Hayward's Ho. Roch —2A 8
Hazel Av. Maid —6F 29
Hazel Gro. Chat —1F 15
Hazels, The. Gill —4B 16
Hazelwood Dri. Maid —6E 28
Hazlemere Dri. Gill —3K 9
Hazlitt Dri. Maid —6G 29
Headcorn Rd. Gill —4B 10
Headcorn Rd. Sut V —6K 43
Headingley Rd. Maid —5E 28
Head Race, The. Maid —2G 35
Heaf Gdns. Roy B —2C 28
Heard Way. Sit —4F 21
Hearne Clo. Sit —4G 21
Heather Clo. Chat —5D 14
Heather Clo. Sit —6E 20
Heather Dri. Maid —2A 36
Heathfield. Langl —1K 43
Heathfield Av. Maid —4B 30
Heathfield Clo. Chat —2F 15
Heathfield Clo. Maid —4A 30
Heathfield Rd. Maid —4A 30
Heath Gro. Maid —2D 34
Heathorn St. Maid —6A 30
Heath Rd. Cox & Lin —2F 41
Heath Rd. Langl —1K 43
Heath Rd. Maid —1C 34
Heath Rd. W Far & E Far —7B 34
Heathside Av. Cox —1F 41
Heath, The. E Mal —6F 27
Hedgerow, The. Weav —6D 30
Hedges, The. Maid —4K 29
Hedley St. Maid —6K 29
(in two parts)
Hellyer Ct. Roch —4A 8
Hempstead La. Bap —6J 21
Hempstead Rd. Hem —6K 15
Hempstead Valley Dri. Hem —3A 16
Hempstead Valley Shop. Cen. Hem —6A 16
Henbane Clo. Weav —6D 30
Hendry Ho. Chatt —1C 4
Hendy Rd. Snod —2D 22
Hengist Ct. Maid —7K 29
Henley Bus. Pk. Roch —1B 8
Henley Clo. Chat —3E 14
Henley Clo. Gill —1D 16
Henley Fields. Weav —5D 30
Henry St. Chat —5F 9
Henry St. Gill —7G 11
Hepplewhite M. Chat —1D 24
Herbert Rd. Chat —5E 8
Herbert Rd. Gill —1E 16
Herdsdown. Hoo —2H 5
Hereford Clo. Gill —6D 10
Hereford Rd. Maid —5C 36
Heritage Dri. Gill —7K 9
Heritage Rd. Chat —3E 14
Herman Ter. Chat —5E 8
Hermitage Ct. Maid —6C 28
Hermitage La. Ayle —3C 28
Hermitage La. Bou M —7C 42
Hermitage La. Det —1F 31
Hermitage Rd. High —4E 2
Herne Rd. Gill —6C 10
Heronden Rd. Maid —1E 42
Heron Rd. Lark —2G 27
Heron Way. Chat —4E 14
Hero Wlk. Roch —2A 14
Herts Cres. Loose —2J 41
Herying Clo. Hall —5D 12
Hever Clo. Maid —6E 36
Hever Croft. Roch —3H 7
Hever Pl. Maid —1H 35
Hever Pl. Sit —6A 20
Hewitt Clo. Gill —2K 9
Hextable Clo. Maid —4F 29
Hickory Dell. Hem —3A 16
Higgins La. Chat —3D 8
Higham Clo. Maid —2G 35
Higham Rd. Wain —4B 4
Higham View. S'lng —7C 24
High Bank. Roch —6B 8
High Banks. Loose —7J 35
Highberry. Leyb —1F 27
Highcroft Grn. Maid —1E 42
High Dewar Rd. Gill —1G 17
High Elms. Gill —6E 10
Highfield Clo. Gill —2D 16
Highfield Rd. Gill —2D 16
Highgrove Rd. Chat —4E 14
Highland Rd. Maid —5D 36
Highlands Clo. Roch —3F 7
High Ridge. Gill —7K 9
Highridge Clo. Weav —6E 30
Highsted Rd. Sit —6D 20
High St. Aylesford, Ayle —7H 23
High St. Brompton, Bromp —2E 8
High St. Chatham, Chat —4D 8
(in two parts)
High St. East Malling, E Mal —4H 27
High St. Gillingham, Gill —2G 9
(in four parts)
High St. Halling, Hall —4C 12
High St. Maidstone, Maid —7J 29
High St. Milton Regis, Mil R —3C 20
High St. Newington, N'tn —3E 18
High St. Rainham, Rain —7E 10
High St. Rochester, Roch
(in two parts) —2A 8
High St. Sittingbourne, Sit —5C 20
High St. Snodland, Snod
(in two parts) —2C 22
High St. Strood, Strood —1J 7
High St. Sutton Valence, Sut V —6K 43
High St. Upnor, Upnor —5D 4
High St. West Malling, W Mal —3C 26
High St. Wouldham, Woul —5E 12
High View. High —3E 2
Highview Clo. Maid —4K 35
Highview Dri. Chat —4B 14
Highwoods Clo. High —3E 2
Hilary Gdns. Roch —6H 7
Hilda Rd. Chat —5E 8
Hildenborough Cres. Maid —4E 28
Hillary Rd. Maid —4K 29
Hillborough Gro. Chat —6E 14
Hill Brow. Bear —6F 31
Hill Brow. Sit —7B 20
Hill Chase. Chat —6C 14
Hill Ct. Chatt —3D 4
Hill Crest. Maid —7J 35
Hill Crest Dri. Cux —6E 6
Hillcrest Rd. Chat —6D 8
Hillden Shaw. Maid —4K 35
Hill Grn. Rd. S'bry —7H 17
Hill Rd. Roch —6J 7
Hill Rd. Woul —4G 13
Hillshaw Cres. Roch —3F 7
Hillside. Roch —6J 7
Hillside Av. Roch —7K 3
Hillside Ct. Roch —1J 7
Hillside Ct. W'bury —5F 33
Hillside Rd. Chat —4E 8
Hill's Ter. Chat —5D 8
Hilltop. Hunt —2A 40
Hill Top Cotts. Langl —3H 41
Hilltop Rd. Roch —6A 4
Hill View Way. Chat —4C 14
Hillyfield Clo. Roch —6H 3
Hilton Dri. Sit —3K 19
Hilton Rd. Cli —1K 3
Hinde Clo. Sit —2D 20
Hines Ter. Chat —7G 9
Hinton Cres. Hem —3A 16
Hoath Clo. Gill —2B 16

A-Z Maidstone, Chatham, Gillingham & Rochester 49

Hoath La.—Linden Clo.

Hoath La. Gill —2B 16
Hoath Way. Gill —2B 16
Hobart Gdns. Sit —5A 20
Hockers Clo. Det —3F 31
Hockers La. Weav —5E 30
Hodgson Cres. Snod —1C 22
Hog Hill. Bear —7G 31
Holborn La. Chat —3D 8
Holborough M. Snod —1C 22
Holborough Rd. Snod —2C 22
Holcombe Rd. Chat —6D 8
Holcombe Rd. Roch —5A 8
Holder Clo. Chat —3G 15
Holding St. Gill —7F 11
Holland Ho. Roch —4B 8
Holland Rd. Chat —5C 14
Holland Rd. Maid —6K 29
Hollands Clo. Shorne —4A 2
(in two parts)
Hollingbourne Hill. Holl —1G 39
Hollingbourne Rd. Gill —5C 10
Hollingworth Rd. Maid —7E 36
Hollow La. H'lip —4A 18
Hollow La. Snod —3B 22
Hollybank Hill. Sit —5C 20
Holly Clo. Chat —7G 9
Holly Clo. Gill —2J 9
Hollycroft. Cux —6E 6
Holly Farm Rd. Otham —6H 37
Holly Rd. Roch —2G 7
Holly Rd. Wain —5B 4
Hollytree Dri. High —4D 2
Holly Vs. Bear —7H 31
(off Street, The)
Holly Vs. W Far —6A 34
Hollywood La. Wain —5A 4
Holmesdale Clo. Loose —2J 41
Holm Mill La. H'shm —6J 39
Holmoaks. Gill —6E 10
Holmoaks. Maid —6B 30
Holmside. Gill —6J 9
Holt Wood Av. Ayle —3A 28
Holtwood Clo. Gill —4D 16
Holtye Cres. Maid —2A 36
Homefield Dri. Rain —6H 11
Homestead View. B'den —7K 19
Home View. Sit —5F 21
Homewood Av. Sit —6B 20
Honduras Ter. Maid —4K 29
Hone St. Roch —7K 3
Honey Bee Glade. Gill —4E 16
Honey Clo. Hem —4A 16
Honey La. Otham —6G 37
Honeypot Clo. Roch —7K 3
Honeysuckle Clo. Chat —5C 14
Honeysuckle Clo. Hem —5K 15
Honeysuckle Ct. Sit —4F 21
Hoo Comn. Chatt —3E 4
Hook Clo. Chat —4C 14
Hook La. H'shm —6K 39
Hook Rd. Snod —2B 22
Hoo Marina Pk. Hoo —4J 5
Hooper's Rd. Roch —4A 8
Hoo Rd. Wain —4B 4
Hope Cotts. Maid —7K 35
Hope St. Chat —5E 8
Hope St. Maid —5J 29
Hopewell Dri. Chat —1G 15
Hornbeam Av. Chat —7F 15
Hornbeam Clo. Lark —2J 27
Horseshoe Clo. Weav —6D 30
Horseshoes La. Langl —1J 43
Horseshore Clo. Hem —4K 15
Horsewash La. Roch —2A 8
Horsham La. Gill —5J 11
Horsley Rd. Roch —4K 7
Horsted Av. Chat —7C 8
Horsted Retail Pk. Chat —3B 14
Horsted Way. Roch —2B 14
Horton Downs. Down —3E 36
Horwood Clo. Roch —1K 13
Hospital La. Roch —4C 8
Hospital Rd. Holl —4F 39
Hostier Clo. Hall —5D 12
Hotel Rd. Gill —6A 10
Hothfield Rd. Rain —7F 11
Houghton Av. Hem —6B 16
Howard Av. Roch —4B 8
Howard Av. Sit —3B 20
Howard Dri. Maid —5E 28
Howard Rd. E Mal —3G 27
Howbury Wlk. Gill —5D 16
Howlsmere Clo. Hall —5D 12
Hubbard's La. Bou M —3K 41
Hubble Dri. Maid —5D 36
Huckleberry Clo. Chat —6F 15
Hudson Clo. Gill —7C 10
Hughes Dri. Wain —5B 4
Hugh Price Clo. Murs —4G 21
Hulkes La. Roch —4C 8
Humber Cres. Roch —1H 7
Humber Ho. Maid —4D 36
Hunstanton Clo. Gill —6E 16
Huntersfield Clo. Chat —1G 25
Hunters Way. Gill —7J 9
Hunters Way W. Chat —6H 9
Huntingdon Wlk. Maid —5D 36
Huntington Rd. Cox —2E 40
Hunton Hill. Hunt —4C 40
Hunton Rd. Yald —7C 40
Huntsford Clo. Gill —4D 16
Huntsman La. Maid —7A 30
(in two parts)
Huntsmans Clo. Chat —7C 8
Huntsmans Clo. Ct. Chat —7B 8
Hunt St. Nett & W Far —7F 33
Hurricane Rd. W Mal —1A 32
Hurst Clo. Chat —3C 14
Hurst Hill. Chat —7C 14
Hurstings, The. Maid —2G 35
Hurst Pl. Gill —1F 17
Hurst Way. Maid —2C 34
Hurstwood. Chat —5C 14
Hutchings Clo. Sit —4G 21
Huxley Ct. Roch —4B 8
(off King St.)
Hyacinth Rd. Roch —2F 7
Hybrid Clo. Roch —7B 8
Hyde Rd. Maid —5G 29
Hyperion Dri. Roch —6H 3
Hythe Rd. Sit —4B 20

Iden Rd. Roch —6A 4
Idenwood Clo. Gill —3D 16
Ifield Clo. Maid —5E 36
Illustrious Clo. Chat —4E 14
Imperial Rd. Gill —5G 9
Impton La. Chat —2D 24
Ingleden Clo. Kem —1D 20
Ingle Rd. Chat —6D 8
Inner Lines. Gill —2E 8
Institute Rd. Chat —4E 8
Inverness Ho. Maid —5D 36
Invicta Ct. Sit —2D 20
Invicta Vs. Bear —7H 31
Iona Clo. Chat —1H 25
Iona Rd. Maid —5K 35
Iris Clo. Chat —2E 24
Ironside Clo. Chat —1E 14
Irvine Rd. High —4D 2
Island Way W. Chat —6F 5
Islingham Farm Rd. Chatt —4B 4
Ivens Way. H'shm —6K 39
Iversgate Clo. Gill —6F 11
Ivy Pl. Roch —6J 7
Ivy St. Gill —1F 17
Iwade Rd. N'tn —2E 18

Jacklin Clo. Chat —7D 14
Jackson Av. Roch —1C 14
Jackson Clo. Gill —7C 10
Jade Hill. Hall —3C 12
Jamaica Ter. Maid —4K 29
James Rd. Cux —6D 6
James St. Chat —4D 8
(in two parts)
James St. Gill —2G 9
James St. Maid —6K 29
James St. Roch —4A 8
James Whatman Way. Maid —6J 29
Japonica Clo. Chat —7G 15
Jarrett Av. Wain —5A 4
Jarretts Ct. Sit —5F 21
(off Wykeham Rd.)
Jarvis Ho. Maid —4J 29
Jasmine Clo. Chat —5D 14
Jasmine Clo. E Mal —3G 27
Jasmine Rd. E Mal —3G 27
Jasper Av. Roch —6A 8
Javelin Rd. W Mal —1A 32
Jefferson Dri. Gill —7C 10
Jeffery St. Gill —2G 9
Jeffrey St. Maid —6K 29
Jeffries Cotts. Maid —2A 40
Jellicoe Pavilion. Roy B —3C 28
Jenkins Dale. Chat —5D 8
Jenkins Dri. Maid —7D 36
Jenner Rd. Roch —4A 8
Jenner Way. Eccl —4H 23
Jennifer Ct. Hoo —2J 5
Jerome Rd. Lark —6B 22
Jersey Rd. Roch —1J 7
Jessica M. Sit —2C 20
Jeyes Rd. Gill —4G 9
Jezreels Rd. Gill —6H 9
Jiniwin Rd. Roch —2B 14
Johannesburg Ho. Maid —7D 36
Johnson Av. Chat —1F 9
Johnson Rd. Sit —5B 20
John St. Maid —5K 29
John St. Roch —4A 8
Joiners Ct. Chat —6F 9
Jordan Clo. Maid —7D 36
Jubilee St. Sit —4C 20
Jubilee Ter. Gill —2G 9
Judkins Clo. Chat —3G 15
Junction Rd. Gill —4H 9
Juniper Clo. Chat —5E 14
Juniper Clo. Maid —5E 28

Katherine Ct. Chat —7F 15
Keats Rd. Lark —7B 22
Keefe Clo. Chat —1B 24
Keel Ct. Roch —7B 4
Keepers Cotts. Det —5H 31
Kellaway Rd. Chat —7E 14
Kelley Dri. Gill —1G 9
Kelly Ho. Roch —2A 14
Kemp Clo. Chat —5C 14
Kemps Wharf Rd. Gill —5F 11
Kempton Clo. Chat —6G 15
(in two parts)
Kemsley St. Rd. Bred —7B 16
Kendal Pl. Maid —4B 36
Kendal Way. Gill —1D 16
Kendon Bus. Pk. Roch —7B 4
Kenilworth Ct. Sit —4A 20
Kenilworth Dri. Gill —2D 16
Kenilworth Gdns. Gill —2D 16
Kenilworth Ho. Maid —2E 34
Kennard Clo. Roch —6H 7
Kennington Clo. Gill —4C 10
Kennington Clo. Maid —5E 36
Kensington Ho. Maid —2D 34
Kent Av. Maid —3B 36
Kent Av. Sit —6B 20
Kent Clo. Roch —1A 14
Kent Ho. Maid —1K 35
Kent Rd. Hall —3C 12
Kent Rd. Snod —4C 22
Kent St. Mere —2A 32
Kenward Rd. Maid —6F 29
Kenward Rd. Yald —7F 33
Kenwood Av. Chat —5E 14
Kenya Ter. Maid —4K 29
Kenyon Wlk. Gill —6B 16
Kesteven Clo. Hall —4C 12
Kestrel Clo. Sit —7E 20
Kestrel Ho. Gill —3F 9
(off Marlborough Rd.)
Kestrel Rd. Chat —7G 15
Keswick Av. Sit —6G 21
Keswick Dri. Maid —6E 28
Kettle La. E Far —7B 34
Kewlands. Maid —5B 30
Keycol Hill. N'tn —4G 19
Keyes Av. Chat —6D 8
Key St. Sit —4J 19
Khartoum Rd. Chat —3D 8
Khyber Rd. Chat —1E 8
Kilburn Ho. Maid —6K 29
Killick Rd. Hoo —2H 5
Kiln Barn Rd. Dit —3K 27
Kiln Clo. Sit —6E 20
Kilndown Clo. Maid —4F 29
Kimberley Rd. Gill —5H 9
King Arthurs Dri. Roch —6H 3
King Edward Rd. Chat —6D 8
King Edward Rd. Gill —2K 9
King Edward Rd. Maid —2J 35
King Edward Rd. Roch —3A 8
Kingfisher Dri. Chat —2G 15
Kingfisher Rd. Lark —1G 27
King George Rd. Chat —6C 14
King Hill. W Mal —7A 26
Kings Acre. Down —3E 36
King's Av. Roch —5A 8
Kings Bastion. Gill —3E 8
Kings Cotts. Leeds —6A 38
King's Cotts. Nett —6E 32
Kingsdale Ct. Chat —7G 9
Kingsdown Clo. Hem —5A 16
Kingsdown Clo. Maid —7H 29
Kingsgate Clo. Maid —7F 29
Kings Hill Av. King H —7B 26
Kingshill Dri. Hoo —1H 5
(in two parts)
Kingsley Rd. Maid —1K 35
Kings Mill Clo. Sit —4C 20
Kingsnorth Clo. Hoo —1J 5
Kingsnorth Rd. Gill —4C 10
Kings Orchard. Roch —3A 8
Kings Rd. Chat —7H 9
Kings Row. Maid —3K 35
Kingston Av. Maid —4K 35
Kingston Cres. Chat —5F 15
King St. Chat —4E 8
King St. Gill —3G 9
King St. Maid —7K 29
King St. Roch —3A 8
King St. Sit —4C 20
King St. W Mal —3D 26
Kingsway. Chat —7H 9
(in three parts)
Kingswear Gdns. Strood —1A 8
Kingswood Av. Chat —6D 8
Kingswood Rd. Ayle —2B 24
Kingswood Rd. Gill —3H 9
King William Rd. Gill —1G 9
Kinross Clo. Chat —2F 15
Kipling Dri. Lark —6B 22
Kirby Rd. Chatt —2D 4
Kirkdale. Loose —7J 35
Kirkdale Clo. Chat —7H 15
Kirkdale Cotts. Maid —7J 35
Kirkdale Rd. Maid —6J 35
Kirkstone Pl. Maid —6J 35
Kitchener Av. Chat —7D 8
Kitchener Rd. Chatt —2D 4
Kitchener Rd. Roch —7J 3
Kit Hill Av. Chat —6C 14
Knaves Acre Ct. Gill —4D 16
Knight Av. Gill —2H 9
Knightrider St. Maid —1K 35
Knight Rd. Roch —3J 7
(in two parts)
Knights Clo. Hoo —2J 5
Knightsfield Rd. Sit —3B 20
Knights Pk. Ind. Est. Roch —2J 7
Knights Rd. Hoo —2H 5
Knole Rd. Chat —6G 15
Knott Ct. Maid —5K 29
Knowle Rd. Maid —5K 29
Knowle Rd. Woul —5E 12
Knowlton Gdns. Maid —2E 34
Kyetop Wlk. Gill —3D 16

Laburnham Pl. Sit —5C 20
Laburnum Dri. Lark —1H 27
Laburnum Rd. Roch —3G 7
Lacarno Av. Gill —6A 10
Lacey Clo. Langl —1K 43
Laceys La. Lin —5F 41
Ladbrooke Ho. Maid —6K 29
Ladds La. Snod —6A 12
Ladywood Rd. Cux —6D 6
Lake Dri. High —1E 2
Lakelands. Maid —5K 35
Lake Rd. Quar W —4B 28
Laker Rd. Roch —3A 14
Lakeside. Snod —4B 22
Lakeside Pk. Roch —1C 8
Lakeview Clo. Snod —4C 22
Lakewood Dri. Gill —3C 16
Lambarde Clo. Hall —5C 12
Lambard Ho. Maid —6K 29
Lamberhurst Rd. Gill —5B 10
Lamberhurst Rd. Maid —4E 28
Lambert M. Snod —2C 22
Lambes Ct. Gill —4D 16
Lambeth Clo. Chat —5F 15
Lambourne Dri. King H —2A 32
Lambourne Pl. Gill —6G 11
Lambourne Rd. Bear —2E 36
Lambourn Way. Chat —6G 15
Lambsfrith Gro. Hem —6B 16
Lammas Dri. Mil R —3C 20
Lamplighters Clo. Hem —4K 15
Lancashire Rd. Maid —5D 36
Lancaster Ct. Gill —2C 16
Lancaster Way. W Mal —1A 32
Lancelot Av. Roch —2G 7
Lancelot Clo. Roch —2G 7
Lancet La. Maid —6J 35
Lancet Pl. Maid —6J 35
Landor Ct. Hem —6A 16
Land Way. High —3F 3
Landway, The. Bear —1E 36
Langdale Clo. Gill —7C 10
Langdale Rise. Maid —6F 29
Langdon Rd. Roch —4A 8
Langham Gro. Maid —7F 29
Langley Pk. Farm Cotts. Langl —1G 43
Langley Rd. Sit —3D 20
Langton Clo. Maid —6B 30
Lankester Parker Rd. Roch —3A 14
Lansdowne Av. Maid —6B 36
Lansdowne Ct. Chat —4D 8
Lansdowne Rd. Chat —6C 8
Lansdown Rd. Sit —5G 21
Lapins La. King H —2A 32
La Providence. Roch —3A 8
Larch Clo. Lark —1J 27
Larchcroft. Chat —5E 14
Larches, The. High —4E 2
Larch Wood Clo. Chat —1H 25
Larkfield Av. Gill —4J 9
Larkfield Av. Sit —3C 20
Larkfield Clo. Lark —2H 27
Larkfield Rd. Lark —2H 27
Larkfield Trad. Est. Lark —5D 22
Larkin Clo. Roch —5K 3
Larkspur Clo. E Mal —2H 27
Larkspur Rd. Chat —5C 14
Larkspur Rd. E Mal —2G 27
Laser Quay. Roch —1B 8
Latimer Pl. Gill —1G 9
Launder Way. Maid —2H 35
Laura Pl. Roch —6H 7
Laurel Rd. Gill —1G 9
Laurels, The. Maid —2F 35
Laurel Wlk. Gill —3E 16
Laurie Gray Av. Chat —1B 24
Lavenda Clo. Hem —5A 16
Lavender Clo. Chat —5C 14
Lavender Clo. E Mal —3G 27
Lavender Ct. Sit —6E 20
Lavender Rd. E Mal —3G 27
Lavenders Rd. W Mal —5D 26
Lavender Wlk. E Mal —3G 27
Laverstoke Rd. All —3F 29
Lawn Clo. Chat —6F 9
Lawrence Clo. Maid —5K 35
Lawrence St. Gill —3G 9
Lawson Ct. Gill —2K 9
Laxey, The. Tovil —2H 35
Laxton Clo. Bear —1E 36
Laxton Dri. Cha S —4F 43
Laxton Way. Sit —3B 20
Layfield Rd. Gill —1K 9
Leafy Glade. Gill —3B 16
Leake Ho. Roch —7A 8
Leander Rd. Roch —2A 14
Leander Wlk. Roch —2A 14
Leeds Rd. Langl —3J 43
Leeds Sq. Gill —5B 10
Lee Rd. Snod —1B 22
Leet Clo. Gill —2J 9
Leeward Rd. Roch —7A 8
Leicester Rd. Maid —5C 36
Leigh Av. Maid —6A 36
Leigh Rd. Wain —4A 4
Leigh Ter. Tstn —3H 33
Leitch Row. Gill —1E 8
(off Admiralty Ter.)
Lendrim Clo. Gill —2E 8
(off Westcourt St.)
Leney Cotts. Up H'lng —4A 12
Leney Rd. W'bury —5F 33
Lenfield Av. Maid —7A 30
Lenham Way. Gill —5A 10
Lennox Row. Gill —1E 8
Lenside Dri. Bear —2F 37
Leonard Clo. Maid —5E 28
Leonard Rd. Chat —5F 9
Leopold Rd. Chat —5E 8
Lesley Pl. Maid —6H 29
Leslie Rd. Gill —1H 9
Lested La. Cha S —3G 43
Lester Rd. Chat —5E 8
Letchworth Av. Chat —7D 8
Lewis Av. Gill —6B 10
Lewis Ct. Dri. Bou M —2A 42
Leybourne Clo. Chat —7E 14
Leybourne Rd. Roch —7H 3
Leybourne Way. Lark —6A 22
Leyton Av. Gill —7J 9
Libya Ter. Maid —4K 29
Lichfield Clo. Gill —6D 10
Lichfield Ho. Maid —5D 36
Lidsing Rd. Boxl —6F 25
Lilac Cres. Roch —2G 7
Lilac Grn. E Mal —2H 27
Lilac Rd. Roch —3G 7
Lilieburn. Leyb —1E 26
Lilk Hill. Bear —1G 37
Lillechurch Rd. High —1H 3
Lime Ct. Gill —6C 16
Lime Cres. E Mal —4H 27
Lime Gro. Sit —5E 20
Limetree Clo. Chat —1F 15
Lincoln Clo. Roch —2F 7
Lincoln Rd. Maid —4B 36
Linden Clo. Sit —6B 20

50 A-Z Maidstone, Chatham, Gillingham & Rochester

Montfort Rd.—Phoenix Cotts.

Montfort Rd. *Chat* —7C **14**
Montfort Rd. *Roch* —1J **7**
Montgomery Av. *Chat* —2E **14**
Montgomery Cotts. *Up H'ing* —4A **12**
Montgomery Rd. *Gill* —4G **9**
Montpelier Ga. *Maid* —6E **28**
Moonstone Dri. *Chat* —7F **15**
Moore St. *Roch* —7J **3**
Mooring Rd. *Roch* —7B **8**
Moor Pk. Clo. *Gill* —1G **17**
Moor St. *Rain* —1H **17**
Morden Ct. *Roch* —4A **8**
Morden St. *Roch* —4A **8**
Morement Rd. *Hoo* —1H **5**
Morgan Rd. *Roch* —7J **3**
Morhen Clo. *Snod* —3A **22**
Morland Dri. *Roch* —6J **3**
Morris Clo. *E Mal* —2G **27**
Morris Ct. Clo. *Bap* —7H **21**
Morse Ho. *Sit* —6G **21**
Mosquito Rd. *W Mal* —1A **32**
Mossbank. *Chat* —6E **14**
Mossy Glade. *Gill* —3E **16**
Mostyn Rd. *Maid* —7B **30**
Mote Av. *Maid* —1A **36**
Mote Rd. *Maid* —1K **35**
Motney Hill Rd. *Gill* —5G **11**
Mountbatten Av. *Chat* —2E **14**
Mountbatten Av. *High* —3E **2**
Mount Cotts. *Bear* —7G **31**
Mount Dri. *Bear* —7G **31**
Mount La. *Bear* —7G **31**
Mount La. *H'lip* —6K **17**
Mt. Pleasant. *Ayle* —7J **23**
Mt. Pleasant. *Chat* —4F **9**
Mt. Pleasant Dri. *Bear* —6F **31**
Mount Rd. *Chat* —5D **8**
Mount Rd. *Roch* —6J **7**
Mountsfield Clo. *Maid* —6G **29**
Mount, The. *Chat* —4D **8**
Mountview. *B'den* —7K **19**
Moyle Clo. *Gill* —5D **16**
Mozart Ct. *Chat* —5C **8**
Muddy La. *Sit* —7F **21**
Muir Rd. *Maid* —1K **35**
Mulberry Clo. *Hem* —5A **16**
Mulberry Ct. *Maid* —6A **30**
Munn's La. *H'lip* —3A **18**
Murrain Dri. *Down* —3F **37**
Murray Rd. *Roch* —6A **4**
Murston Rd. *Sit* —6F **21**
Museum Av. *Maid* —6J **29**
Museum St. *Maid* —7J **29**
Musgrave Rd. *Sit* —3D **20**
Musket La. *Holl* —2B **38**
(in two parts)
Mustang Rd. *W Mal* —1A **32**
Mynn Cres. *Bear* —7F **31**
Myrtle Cres. *Chat* —4D **14**

Nagpur Ho. *Maid* —7D **36**
Nags Head La. *Roch* —4B **8**
Napier Clo. *Sit* —5A **20**
Napier Ct. *Maid* —4J **29**
Napier Rd. *Gill* —4H **9**
Napwood Clo. *Gill* —3D **16**
Nares Rd. *Gill* —5D **16**
Nash Clo. *Chat* —7G **15**
Nashenden Farm La. *Roch* —7H **7**
Nashenden La. *Roch* —6H **7**
Natal Rd. *Chat* —6E **8**
Nativity Clo. *Sit* —5C **20**
Naylor's Cotts. *Gill* —7B **16**
Neale St. *Chat* —6D **8**
Neath Ct. *Maid* —4D **36**
Nelson Ct. *Chat* —7G **9**
Nelson Ho. *Maid* —7E **36**
Nelson Rd. *Gill* —4H **9**
Nelson Rd. *Woul* —5E **12**
Nelson Ter. *Chat* —7G **9**
Nelson Wlk. *Sit* —4K **19**
Neptune Bus. Ct. *Roch* —1C **8**
Neptune Clo. *Roch* —1C **8**
Neptune Way. *Roch* —2C **8**
Nestor Ct. *Tstn* —4H **33**
Netley Clo. *Maid* —5C **30**
Nettlestead La. *Mere* —6B **32**
Nevill Ct. *W Mal* —2D **26**
Neville Clo. *Maid* —3A **30**
Neville Rd. *Chat* —6C **8**
Nevill Pl. *Snod* —3C **22**
Nevill Rd. *Snod* —3C **22**
Newark Rd. *W'sham* —3H **21**
Newark Ter. *Roch* —1K **7**
Newark Yd. *Roch* —1K **7**
New Barns Rd. *Maid* —3K **29**
Newbridge Av. *Sit* —2C **20**
Newbury Av. *Maid* —4F **29**
Newchurch Rd. *Maid* —3K **35**
*New Convenant Pl. Roch —4B **8***
(off New Rd.)
New Covenant Pl. *Roch* —4B **8**
New Cut. *Chat* —4D **8**
New Cut. *E Far* —5G **35**
New Cut Rd. *Weav* —7C **30**
New Delhi Ho. *Maid* —7D **36**
Neweden Clo. *Maid* —5B **30**
Newenden Rd. *Wain* —5A **4**
New Hythe Bus. Pk. *Lark* —7D **22**
New Hythe Ho. *Lark & Ayle* —6D **22**
New Hythe La. *Lark & Ayle* —2H **27**
Newington Enterprise Cen. *N'tn* —1E **18**
Newington Ind. Est. *H'lip* —3B **18**
Newington Wlk. *Maid* —5B **30**
*New Inn Cotts. E Far —5F **35***
(off Forge La.)
Newitt Rd. *Hoo* —2J **5**
Newlands Av. *Sit* —5K **19**
Newlyn Ct. *Maid* —7K **29**
Newman Dri. *Kem* —1D **20**
Newnham Clo. *Gill* —6C **10**
Newnham St. *Chat* —5F **9**
New Rd. *Burh* —1H **23**
New Rd. *Chat* —4D **8**
New Rd. *Dit* —2K **27**
New Rd. *E Mal* —3H **27**
New Rd. *Langl* —6H **37**
New Rd. *Roch* —4B **8**
New Rd. Av. *Chat* —4C **8**
New Rd. Bus. Est. *Dit* —3J **27**
New Stairs. *Chat* —2D **8**
New St. *Chat* —5C **8**
Newton Clo. *Chat* —7G **15**
Newton Clo. *Maid* —1H **35**
New Vs. *Maid* —5F **35**
Nicholas Clo. *Barm* —1D **34**
Nicklaus Dri. *Chat* —6D **14**
Nickleby Clo. *Roch* —6A **8**
Nightingale Clo. *Gill* —3E **16**
Nightingale Clo. *Lark* —1G **27**
Nile Rd. *Gill* —4G **9**
Nine Acres Rd. *Cux* —5D **6**
Niven Clo. *Wain* —5A **4**
Norah La. *High* —3D **2**
Norfolk Clo. *Chat* —6G **15**
Norfolk Clo. *Gill* —6D **10**
Norfolk Rd. *Maid* —4B **36**
Norman Clo. *Gill* —5B **16**
Norman Clo. *Maid* —5A **30**
Norman Clo. *Roch* —4H **7**
Norman Rd. *Snod* —4C **22**
Norman Rd. *W Mal* —2B **26**
Norreys Rd. *Gill* —2E **16**
Norrington Rd. *Maid* —6K **35**
N. Bank Clo. *Roch* —3H **7**
Northbank Ho. *Roch* —2B **8**
Northbourne Rd. *Gill* —4B **10**
Northcote Rd. *Roch* —1J **7**
North Ct. *Maid* —3K **35**
North Cres. *Cox* —1G **41**
N. Dane Way. *Chat* —2G **15**
Northdown Clo. *Maid* —4A **30**
N. Downs Ho. *Up H'ing* —4A **12**
Northfields. *Maid* —2C **34**
Northfleet Clo. *Maid* —6D **30**
N. Folly Rd. *E Far* —2C **40**
North Ga. *Roch* —2A **8**
Northleigh Clo. *Maid* —6K **35**
Northpoint Bus. Est. *Roch* —7C **4**
N. Pole Rd. *E Mal & Barm* —2G **33**
North Rd. *Cha S* —4H **43**
North Rd. *Chat* —1E **8**
North St. *Barm* —1B **34**
North St. *Sit* —2C **20**
North St. *Strood* —1K **7**
North St. *Sut V* —6K **43**
North Ter. *Chatt* —1D **4**
Northumberland Av. *Gill* —7F **11**
*Northumberland Ct. Maid —5C **36***
(off Northumberland Rd.)
Northumberland Rd. *Maid* —5B **36**
North View. *Maid* —3A **36**
N. View Cotts. *Maid* —5F **35**
North Way. *Maid* —4A **30**
Norton Gro. *Chat* —5C **14**
Norton Rd. *Cha S* —4H **43**
Norway Ter. *Maid* —4K **29**
Norwich Clo. *Roch* —2F **7**
Norwich Ho. *Maid* —5C **36**
Norwood Wlk. *Sit* —4K **19**
Norwood Wlk. E. *Sit* —4A **20**
Norwood Wlk. W. *Sit* —3K **19**
Nottingham Av. *Maid* —5C **36**
Nottingham Wlk. *Roch* —2F **7**
Nursery Av. *Bear* —1G **37**
Nursery Av. *Maid* —5E **28**
Nursery Gdns. *Hoo* —2J **5**
Nursery Rd. *Dit* —2K **27**
Nursery Rd. *Gill* —1D **16**
Nutfield Clo. *Chat* —1F **15**
Nutfields *Sit* —6F **21**
Nutwood Clo. *Weav* —7D **30**

Oakapple Ho. *Maid* —1D **34**
Oakapple La. *Barm* —1C **34**
Oak Av. *Gill* —2J **9**
*Oak Cotts. Bear —7H **31***
(off Green, The)
Oak Cotts. *Langl* —2A **42**
Oak Dri. *High* —4D **2**
Oak Dri. *Lark* —1H **27**
Oakfields. *Sit* —6A **20**
Oakhurst Clo. *Chat* —6D **14**
Oakland Clo. *Chat* —6D **14**
Oak La. *Upc* —2J **17**
Oakleigh Clo. *W'slde* —7C **14**
Oak Rd. *Roch* —2G **7**
Oak Rd. *Sit* —5G **21**
Oaks Bus. Village, The. *Chat* —1G **25**
Oaks Dene. *Chat* —2D **24**
Oaks, The. *Ayle* —2B **28**
Oak Ter. *Chat* —7E **14**
Oak Tree Av. *Maid* —5B **36**
*Oaktree Ho. Sit —6F **21***
(off Woodberry Dri.)
Oakum Ct. *Chat* —6F **9**
Oakwood Ct. *Maid* —1G **35**
Oakwood Rd. *Maid* —1F **35**
Oast Ct. *Sit* —7C **20**
Oastview. *Rain* —1G **17**
Ocelot Ct. *Chat* —5F **9**
Octavia Ct. *Chat* —6F **15**
Odiham Dri. *Maid* —4F **29**
Offham Rd. *W Mal* —4A **26**
Officer's Rd. *Chat* —7F **5**
*Officers Ter. Chat —2D **8***
(off Church La.)
Old Barn Clo. *Hem* —3K **15**
Old Barn Rd. *Leyb* —1E **26**
Old Carriage Way, The. *Gill* —5K **15**
Old Castle Wlk. *Gill* —5D **16**
Old Chatham Rd. *Blue B* —3B **24**
Old Chatham Rd. *S'lng* —5C **24**
Oldchurch Ct. *Maid* —1H **35**
Old Chu. Rd. *Burh* —7E **12**
Old Cotts. *Maid* —2H **35**
Old Dri. *Maid* —6J **35**
Oldfield Clo. *Gill* —1D **16**
Oldfield Clo. *Maid* —3D **36**
Old Ho. La. *H'lip* —5A **18**
Old Loose Clo. *Loose* —1J **41**
Old Loose Hill. *Loose* —1J **41**
*Old Manor Cotts. Bear —7H **31***
(off Green, The)
Old Mill Cotts. *Holl* —3A **38**
Old Mill La. *Ayle* —7A **24**
Old Mill Rd. *Holl* —4A **38**
Old Oast Bus. Cen., The. *Ayle* —2D **28**
Old Orchard La. *Leyb* —2E **26**
Old Orchard, The. *Rain* —7G **11**
Old Parsonage Ct. *W Mal* —4D **26**
Old Pattens La. *Roch* —5B **8**
Old Rd. *Chat* —4D **8**
Old Rd. *W'bury* —5C **32**
Old Ryarsh La. *W Mal* —2C **26**
Old School Clo. *Burh* —1H **23**
Old School Ct. *Chatt* —3D **4**
Old Tovil Rd. *Maid* —2J **35**
Old Trafford Clo. *Maid* —5E **28**
Old Tree La. *Bou M* —2B **42**
Old Vinters Rd. *Maid* —7A **30**
Old Watling St. *Roch* —7D **2**
Old Well Ct. *Maid* —2H **35**
Oliver Clo. *Chat* —6F **9**
Olivers Cotts. *Bear* —7H **31**
Oliver Twist Clo. *Roch* —4K **7**
Olivine Clo. *Chat* —2E **24**
Olliffe Clo. *Chat* —7D **14**
Onslow Rd. *Roch* —5B **8**
Opal Grn. *Chat* —7F **15**
Orache Dri. *Weav* —6D **30**
Orange Ter. *Roch* —3B **8**
Orbit Clo. *Chat* —2E **24**
Orchard Av. *Ayle* —2B **28**
Orchard Av. *Roch* —6H **3**
Orchard Bank. *Cha S* —4G **43**
Orchard Bus. Cen. *All* —3F **29**
Orchard Clo. *Cox* —2F **41**
Orchard Clo. *Langl* —1K **43**
Orchard Clo. *Maid* —1K **35**
Orchard Cotts. *Maid* —4D **34**
Orchard Dri. *N'tn* —4C **18**
Orchard Dri. *Weav* —1D **36**
Orchard Gro. *Dit* —1J **27**
Orchard Ind. Est. *Maid* —2E **42**
Orchard Pl. *Maid* —1H **35**
Orchard Pl. *Sit* —6E **20**
Orchard St. *Gill* —2E **16**
Orchard St. *Maid* —1K **35**
Orchard, The. *Bear* —7G **31**
Orchard Vs. *Chat* —5D **8**
Orchard Way. *Snod* —3B **22**
Orchid Clo. *Roch* —2E **6**
Orchid Pk. *Roch* —5B **8**
Ordnance St. *Chat* —5C **8**
Ordnance Ter. *Chat* —4C **8**
Oriel Ho. *Roch* —3A **8**
Oriole Way. *Lark* —1G **27**
Orion Rd. *Roch* —2A **14**
Ormsby Grn. *Gill* —6E **16**
Orpines, The. *W'bury* —5G **33**
Orwell Clo. *Lark* —7B **22**
Orwell Ho. *Maid* —4D **36**
Orwell Spike. *W Mal* —6B **26**
Osbourne Dri. *Det* —1H **31**
Osbourne Rd. *Gill* —3H **9**
Osprey Ct. *Sit* —6E **20**
Osprey Wlk. *Lark* —2G **27**
Ostlers Clo. *Snod* —2C **22**
Ostlers Ct. *High* —1E **2**
Otham La. *Bear* —2H **37**
Otham St. *Otham & Bear* —5G **37**
Otterbourne Pl. *Maid* —3D **36**
Otterham Quay La. *Rain* —1H **17**
Otteridge Rd. *Bear* —1F **37**
Otway St. *Chat* —5E **8**
Otway St. *Gill* —2H **9**
Otway Ter. *Chat* —5E **8**
Owen Clo. *E Mal* —3G **27**
Oxford Rd. *Gill* —5H **9**
Oxford Rd. *Maid* —4C **36**
Oxford St. *Snod* —2C **22**
Oxley Shaw La. *Leyb* —2E **26**
Oyster Clo. *Sit* —3C **20**

Packer Pl. *Chat* —1E **14**
Paddock Cotts. *Woul* —4E **12**
Paddocks, The. *Hem* —4A **16**
Paddock, The. *Chat* —4D **8**
Pad's Hill. *Maid* —7K **29**
Padsole La. *Maid* —7K **29**
*Padstow Mnr. Gill —2G **9***
(off Arden St.)
Paget Row. *Gill* —3G **9**
Paget St. *Gill* —3F **9**
Pagitt St. *Chat* —6C **8**
Palace Av. *Maid* —7K **29**
Palace Ct. *Chat* —6H **9**
Palace Ind. Est. *Maid* —1E **42**
Palm Cotts. *Maid* —1H **41**
Palmer Rd. *Maid* —5G **29**
Palmerston Rd. *Chat* —1D **14**
Palmerston Wlk. *Sit* —5G **21**
Pankhurst Rd. *Hoo* —1H **5**
Panteny La. *Bap* —7J **21**
Panton Clo. *Chat* —5G **15**
Papion Gro. *Chat* —7C **14**
Papyrus Way. *Lark* —6D **22**
Parham Rd. *Chat* —6D **8**
Park Av. *Gill* —6H **9**
Park Av. *Lin* —3H **41**
Park Av. *Maid* —5A **30**
Park Av. *Sit* —7C **20**
Park Barn Rd. *Broom* —7C **38**
Park Cres. *Chat* —1D **14**
Parker Clo. *Gill* —4E **16**
Park Farm. *Dit* —3J **27**
Parkfield Rd. *Gill* —6F **11**
Parkfields. *Roch* —1E **6**
Park Ho. *Maid* —5A **30**
Park La. *Bou M* —3C **42**
Park La. *Maid* —4J **29**
Park Mnr. *Gill* —3G **9**
Park Pale. *Roch* —7B **2**
Park Rd. *Mere* —7A **32**
Park Rd. *Sit* —7C **20**
Park View Clo. *Maid* —3D **36**
Park Way. *Cox* —2F **41**
Park Way. *Maid* —3A **36**
Park Wood Grn. Shop. Cen. *Gill* —4D **16**
Park Wood Pde. *Maid* —7E **36**
Park Wood Trad. Est. *Maid* —1F **43**
Parr Av. *Gill* —2H **9**
Parrs Head M. *Roch* —2A **8**
Parsonage Ct. *W Mal* —3D **26**
Parsonage La. *Bob* —1H **19**
Parsonage La. *Roch* —6A **4**
Partridge Av. *Lark* —7B **22**
Pasley Rd. *Gill* —2E **8**
Pasley Rd. E. *Chat* —1F **9**
Pasley Rd. N. *Chat* —1F **9**
Pasley Rd. W. *Chat* —1E **8**
Patrixbourne Av. *Gill* —6C **10**
Pattens Gdns. *Roch* —6B **8**
Pattens La. *Chat* —6B **8**
Pattens Pl. *Roch* —6B **8**
Pavilion Dri. *Kem* —1D **20**
Pavilion La. *Mere* —4B **32**
Pavings, The. *Holl* —2D **38**
Payne's La. *Maid* —5K **35**
Peace Cotts. *Maid* —6A **40**
Peacock M. *Maid* —7H **29**
Peal Clo. *Hoo* —2J **5**
Pearman Clo. *Gill* —7G **11**
*Pear Tree All. Sit —4C **20***
(off St Paul's St.)
Pear Tree Av. *Dit* —2K **27**
Pear Tree La. *Hem* —1J **15**
Pear Tree La. *Maid* —6A **36**
Peartree La. *Shorne* —6A **2**
Peartree Pl. *High* —4D **2**
Pear Tree Row. *Langl* —7G **37**
Pear Tree Wlk. *N'tn* —4C **18**
Peckham Clo. *Roch* —7A **4**
Peel Dri. *Sit* —5G **21**
Peel St. *Maid* —5K **29**
Peel St. Hedges. *Maid* —4K **29**
Peens La. *Bou M* —5B **42**
Peggoty Clo. *High* —4D **2**
Pelican Clo. *Roch* —2E **6**
Pelican Ct. *W'bury* —5F **33**
Pemberton Sq. *Roch* —7A **4**
Pembroke. *Chat* —7E **4**
Pembroke Gdns. *Gill* —5E **16**
Pembroke Rd. *Cox* —2E **40**
*Pembury Ct. Sit —5C **20***
(off Pembury St.)
Pembury Gdns. *Maid* —1G **35**
Pembury St. *Sit* —5C **20**
Pembury Way. *Gill* —6E **10**
Penenden Ct. *Maid* —4A **30**
Penenden Heath Rd. *Maid* —4B **30**
Penenden St. *Maid* —5K **29**
Penfold Clo. *Chat* —2F **15**
Penfold Clo. *Maid* —7D **36**
Penfold Hill. *Leeds* —4C **38**
Penfold Way. *Maid* —6J **35**
Penguin Clo. *Roch* —2F **7**
Penhurst Clo. *Weav* —6E **30**
Pennant Rd. *Roch* —2A **14**
Penn Clo. *Sit* —7F **21**
Pennine Way. *Down* —3F **37**
*Penryn Mnr. Gill —2G **9***
(off Skinner St.)
Penshurst Clo. *Gill* —6E **10**
Penstocks, The. *Maid* —2G **35**
Pentagon Cen. *Chat* —4D **8**
Pepper All. *Maid* —3H **29**
Pepy's Way. *Roch* —1H **7**
Peregrine Dri. *Sit* —6E **20**
Peregrine Rd. *King H* —2B **32**
*Perie Row. Gill —2E **8***
(off Middle St.)
Perimeter Rd. *Lark* —7E **22**
Periwinkle Clo. *Sit* —4C **20**
Perryfield St. *Maid* —5J **29**
Perry St. *Chat* —5C **8**
Perry St. *Maid* —5J **29**
Perth Gdns. *Sit* —5A **20**
Pested Bars Rd. *Bou M* —7B **36**
Peterborough Gdns. *Roch* —2E **6**
Peters Works. *Woul* —6E **12**
Petham Grn. *Gill* —5C **10**
Peverel Dri. *Bear* —7E **30**
Peverel Grn. *Gill* —5D **16**
Pheasant La. *Maid* —5A **36**
Pheasant Rd. *Chat* —6G **9**
Phillippa Ct. *Mil R* —2C **20**
Phillips Ct. *Gill* —6B **10**
*Phoenix Cotts. W'bury —6E **32***
(off Maidstone Rd.)

52 A-Z Maidstone, Chatham, Gillingham & Rochester

Phoenix Dri.—St Edmunds Way

Phoenix Dri. W'bury —5F 33
Phoenix Ind. Est. Strood —1B 8
Phoenix Pk. Bus. Cen. Maid —1E 42
Phoenix Rd. Chat —7F 15
Phoenix Wharf. Roch —1B 8
Pickering St. Maid —7K 35
Pickwick Cres. Roch —6A 8
Pier App. Rd. Gill —1H 9
Pier Pl. Roch —4E 4
Pier Rd. Gill —1H 9
Pier Rd. Ind. Est. Gill —1H 9
Pikefields. Gill —6C 10
Pikey La. E Mal —6E 26
Pilgrim Cotts. Up H'lng —4A 12
Pilgrims View. S'lng —7C 24
Pilgrims View. Snod —2B 22
Pilgrims Way. Boxl & Holl —6F 25
Pilgrims Way. Burh —3J 23
Pilgrims Way. Cux —5E 6
Pilgrims Way. Up H'ling —6A 12
Pilot Rd. Roch —1A 14
Pimpernal Clo. Bear —7G 31
Pimpernel Way. Chat —5C 14
Pimps Ct. Cotts. Maid —6H 35
Pine Clo. Lark —1H 27
Pine Cotts. All —3H 29
Pine Gro. Hem —3A 16
Pine Gro. Maid —5A 30
Pine Ho. Chat —4D 14
Pine Lodge. Maid —1F 35
Pine Lodge Cvn. Pk. Holl —2A 38
Pine Pl. Tovil —3H 35
Pine Rd. Roch —2H 7
Pinewood Dri. Chat —2H 25
Pintails, The. St Mi —6F 5
Piper's Cotts. Maid —1H 41
Pippin Clo. Cox —3E 40
Pippin Clo. Sit —3B 20
Pippin Way. King H —2B 32
Pippon Croft. Hem —3A 16
Pirbright Clo. Chat —7H 15
Pitt Rd. Kgswd —2K 43
Pitt Rd. Maid —3E 34
Pizien Well Rd. W'bury —6B 32
Place La. H'lip —4K 17
Plains Av. Maid —3A 36
Plaistow Sq. Maid —5B 30
Plantation La. Bear —7F 31
Plantation Rd. Gill —2A 10
Platters Farm Lodge. Gill —2D 16
Platters, The. Gill —1C 16
Platt, The. Sut V —6K 43
Playstool Clo. N'tn —3D 18
Playstool Rd. N'tn —3C 18
Pleasant Courts. Det —2F 31
Pleasant Row. Chat —2E 8
Pleasant Row. Roch —3A 8
Pleasant Valley La. Maid —1E 40
Plomley Clo. Gill —5D 16
Plough Cotts. Langl —3J 43
Ploughmans Way. Chat —1E 24
Ploughmans Way. Gill —3E 16
Plough Wents Rd. Cha S —3E 42
Plover Clo. Chat —1H 25
Plover Rd. Lark —1G 27
Pluckley Clo. Gill —5C 10
Plumpton Wlk. Maid —6E 36
Plumtree Gro. Hem —5A 16
Plumtrees. Maid —2D 34
Poachers Clo. Chat —4G 15
Pochard Clo. St Mi —6F 5
Podkin Wood. Chat —2D 24
Polhill Dri. Chat —7D 14
Police Sta. Rd. W Mal —3D 26
Pond Dri. Sit —7E 20
Pondfield La. Shorne —6A 2
Pope St. Maid —2F 35
Poplar Clo. Roch —3H 7
Poplar Gro. Maid —6E 28
Poplar Rd. Roch —3G 7
Poplicans Rd. Cux —5D 6
Poppy Clo. Gill —3J 9
Poppy Clo. Maid —1G 35
Porchester Clo. Maid —6K 35
Port Clo. Chat —6F 15
Porters Wlk. Langl —1K 43
Portland Av. Sit —5G 21
Portland Pl. Snod —2C 22
Portland Rd. Gill —2J 9
Portland Rd. Woul —5E 12
Portland St. Chat —6F 9
Port Rise. Chat —5D 8
Portsdown Clo. Maid —2E 34
Portsmouth Clo. Roch —2F 7
Post Barn Rd. Chat —6D 8
Postley Commercial Cen. Maid —2K 35
Postley Ind. Cen. Maid —3K 35
Postley Rd. Maid —3K 35
Postmill Dri. Maid —3J 35
Pottery Rd. Hoo —2H 5
Potyn Ho. Roch —4A 8
Poulsen Ct. Sit —6F 21
Pout Rd. Snod —3B 22
Povey Av. Wain —5A 4
Powell Clo. Ayle —7J 23
Powlett Rd. Roch —6A 4
Pratling St. Ayle —7K 23
Precinct, The. Roch —3A 8
Premier Pde. Ayle —2B 28
Prentis Clo. Sit —4A 20
Prentis Quay. Sit —4C 20
Preston Av. Gill —7J 9
Preston Way. Gill —6C 10
Pretoria Ho. Maid —7D 36
Pretoria Rd. Chat —6D 8
Pretoria Rd. Gill —5H 9
Pridmore Rd. Snod —2B 22
Priestfield Rd. Gill —3J 9
Priestfields. Roch —5K 7
Priestley Dri. Lark —6B 22
Primrose Av. Gill —4B 16
Primrose Clo. Chat —2C 14
Primrose Cotts. Maid —4G 37
Primrose Dri. Dit —2A 28
Primrose Rd. Up H'lng —4A 12
Prince Arthur Rd. Gill —2F 9
Prince Charles Av. Chat —5F 15
Prince Charles Av. Sit —7F 21
Princes Av. Chat —6E 14
Princess Mary Av. Chat —1F 9
Princes St. Maid —6K 29
Prince's St. Roch —4A 8
Princes Way. Det —2F 31
Prinys Dri. Gill —5C 16
Priors Dean Clo. Barm —3B 34
Priors Ga. Roch —3A 8
Priory Clo. E Far —4E 34
Priory Ct. Gill —6A 10
Priory Ga. Maid —6K 29
Priory Gro. Dit —2A 28
Priory Rd. Gill —6A 10
Priory Rd. Maid —1K 35
Priory Rd. Roch —2J 7
Priory, The. E Far —4F 35
Progress Est., The. Maid —7F 37
Prospect Av. Roch —7K 3
Prospect Pl. Maid —1H 35
Prospect Pl. Roch —6J 7
Prospect Row. Chat —5E 8
Prospect Row. Gill —2E 8
Provender Way. Weav —6D 30
Providence Cotts. High —5D 2
Providence Pl. Woul —5E 12
Pudding La. Maid —7J 29
Pudding Rd. Rain —1F 17
Pump Clo. Leyb —2E 26
Pump La. Gill —7C 10 (in two parts)
Purbeck Rd. Chat —6C 8
Purser Way. Gill —1G 9
Puttney Dri. Kem —1E 20
Pyrus Clo. Chat —2F 25

Quarries, The. Bou M —1B 42
Quarry Cotts. Langl —1A 42
Quarry Rd. Maid —2K 35
Quarry Sq. Maid —6K 29
Quarry Wood Ind. Est. Ayle —3B 28
Quayside. Chat —7F 5
Queen Anne Rd. Maid —7K 29
Queen Ct. Roch —4A 8
Queendown Av. Gill —4D 16
Queen Elizabeth Sq. Maid —6C 36
Queen Mother Ct., The. Roch —4K 7
Queen's Av. Maid —6G 29
Queen's Av. Snod —2C 22
Queen's Farm Rd. Shorne —1A 2
Queens Ho. Maid —1E 34
Queens Rd. Chat —6H 9
Queens Rd. Gill —4G 9
Queen's Rd. Maid —1E 34
Queen's Rd. Snod —2C 22
Queen St. Chat —4E 8
Queen St. Roch —4A 8 (in two parts)
Queensway. Det —2F 31
Queenswood Rd. Ayle —3B 24
Quern, The. Maid —3H 35
Quested Way. H'shm —6K 39
Quickthorn Cres. Chat —4C 14
Quinell St. Gill —7E 10
Quinion Clo. Chat —2D 24
Quinton Rd. Mil R —2A 20
Quixote Cres. Roch —6K 3

Racefield Clo. Shorne —6A 2
Radleigh Gdns. Chat —7C 8
Raggatt Pl. Maid —2A 36
Ragstone Ct. Dit —3K 27
Ragstone Rd. Bear —2F 37
Railway St. Chat —4C 8
Railway St. Gill —3H 9
Railway St. Ind. Est. Gill —2H 9
Rainham Clo. Maid —3J 35
Rainham Shop. Cen. Rain —7F 11
Raleigh Clo. Chat —3E 14
Ramillies Clo. Chat —4E 14
Rampion Clo. Weav —6D 30
Randall Rd. Chat —7C 8
Randalls Row. Loose —7J 35
Randall St. Maid —5J 29
Randolph Cotts. Roch —6K 3
Randolph Ho. Gill —3G 9
Randolph Rd. Gill —3G 9
Ranscombe Clo. Roch —3F 7
Ratcliffe Highway. Chatt —2E 4
Raven Clo. Lark —2H 27
Ravens Dane Clo. Down —3F 37
Ravenswood Av. Roch —7K 3
Rawdon Rd. Maid —1K 35
Raymer Rd. Maid —3A 30
Reading Ho. Maid —7E 36
Readscroft Rd. Gill —4D 16
Recreation Av. Snod —2C 22
Recreation Clo. Maid —5A 30
Rectory Clo. Snod —2C 22
Rectory Clo. Woul —4E 12
Rectory Grange. Roch —6A 8
Rectory La. Barm —3C 34
Rectory La. Cha S —7H 43
Rectory La. Sut V —6K 43
Rectory La. N. Leyb —1F 27
Rectory La. S. Leyb —1F 27
Rectory Rd. Sit —7F 21
Reculver Wlk. Maid —5E 36
Redbank. Leyb —1F 27
Redbridge Clo. Chat —4G 15
Redcliffe La. Maid —4K 29
Red Cotts. Maid —3H 29
Rede Ct. Rd. Strood —7F 3
Rede Wood Rd. Maid —1B 34
Redfern Av. Gill —3J 9
Red Hill. W'bury —4F 33
Red Ho. Gdns. W'bury —5D 32
Redland Shaw. Roch —7C 8
Redruth Mnr. Gill —2G 9 (off Cross St.)
Redsells Clo. Down —3F 37
Redvers Rd. Chat —6E 8
Redwall Bungalows. Lin —7G 41
Redwall La. Hunt —6D 40
Redwall La. Lin —6H 41
Redwing Clo. Lark —7B 22
Redwing Rd. Chat —3F 15
Redwood Clo. Chat —7F 15
Reeds Ct. Maid —2G 35
Reform Rd. Chat —6F 9
Regency Clo. Gill —6C 16
Regency Ct. Sit —5B 20
Regent Dri. Maid —4K 35
Regent Rd. Gill —4G 9
Reginald Av. Cux —5E 6
Reginald Rd. Maid —1H 35
Regis Cres. Sit —3C 20
Reinden Gro. Down —3E 36
Renown Rd. Chat —7G 15
Repton Way. Chat —5D 14
Reservoir Cotts. Up H'lng —5A 12
Resolution Clo. Chat —4E 14
Restharrow Rd. Weav —7D 30
Retreat Cvn. Pk., The. Nett —6E 32
Revenge Rd. Chat —1G 25
Reynolds Fields. High —1E 2
Rhode Ct. Sit —4A 20
Rhode St. Chat —4E 8
Rhodewood Clo. Down —3F 37
Richard St. Chat —4D 8
Richard St. Roch —5A 8
Richborough Dri. Strood —6J 3
Richmond Clo. Chat —5F 15
Richmond Clo. Upnor —6D 4
Richmond Dri. Sit —2C 20
Richmond Pde. Roch —5B 8
Richmond Rd. Gill —2G 9
Richmond Way. Maid —4K 35
Riddles Rd. Sit —6A 20
Ridgeway Bungalows. Shorne —6B 2
Ridgeway, The. Chat —2C 14
Ridgeway, The. Gill —2G 9
Ridgeway, The. Shorne —6A 2
Ridgway. Maid —2E 34
Ridley Rd. Roch —4K 7
Rigden's Ct. Sit —4C 20
Ringlestone Cres. Maid —3J 29
Ringwood Clo. Gill —1D 16
Ringwood Rd. Maid —4B 36
Ripon Av. Gill —7A 10
Ripon Clo. Gill —5D 10
Ripton Cotts. Tstn —5H 33
Rise, The. B'den —7K 19
Rise, The. Hem —6A 16
Rise, The. Roch —5B 8
Ritch Rd. Snod —2A 22
River Clo. E Far —5E 34
River Dri. Roch —1G 7
Riverhead Clo. Maid —5G 29
Riverhead Clo. Sit —6A 20
Rivers Clo. W'bury —5F 33
Riverside Cvn. Pk. E Far —4D 34
Riverside Est. Roch —2C 8
Riverside View. Ayle —1E 28
River St. Gill —2E 8
River View. Gill —5D 10
River View. Maid —2J 35
River Way. Lark —6C 22
Roach St. Roch —1J 7
Roan Ct. Roch —7H 3
Roberts Clo. Sit —2B 20
Roberts Orchard Rd. Maid —1C 34
Roberts Rd. Gill —1E 16
Roberts Rd. Snod —2B 22
Robin Hood La. W'slde —7D 14
Robin Hood La. Lwr. W'slde —7C 14
Robin Hood La. Up. Blue B —1B 24
Robson Dri. Ayle —1A 28
Robson Dri. Hoo —2H 5
Rocfort Rd. Snod —2C 22
Rochester Av. Roch —4A 8
Rochester Ct. Roch —7C 4
Rochester Cres. Hoo —1H 5
Rochester Ga. Roch —3B 8
Rochester Ho. Maid —5C 36
Rochester Rd. Ayle —7J 23
Rochester Rd. Burh —6F 13
Rochester Rd. Cux —7D 6 (in two parts)
Rochester Rd. Roch & Chat —3A 14
Rochester Rd. Woul —4E 12
Rochester St. Chat —6C 8
Rock Av. Gill —4G 9
Rock Rd. Maid —4K 29
Rock Rd. Sit —6C 20
Rocks Clo. E Mal —5H 27
Rocks Rd., The. E Mal —5H 27
Rocky Hill. Maid —7H 29
Rocky Hill Ter. Maid —7H 29
Roebuck Rd. Roch —3A 8
Roffen Rd. Roch —6A 8
Rolvenden Av. Gill —5C 10
Rolvenden Dri. Sit —4K 19
Rolvenden Rd. Wain —5A 4
Roman Clo. Blue B —1B 24
Roman Heights. Maid —5B 30
Roman Rd. Snod —2B 22
Roman Sq. Sit —6D 20
Roman Way. Roch —4H 7
Romany Ct. Chat —6H 9
Romany Rd. Gill —6B 10
Rome Ter. Chat —4D 8
Romney Clo. Bear —1F 37
Romney Ct. Sit —4B 20
Romney Pl. Maid —7K 29
Romney Rd. Chat —4F 15
Romsey Clo. Roch —7G 3
Ronalds Ct. Sit —5E 20
Rook La. Bob —4G 19
Roonagh Ct. Sit —7C 20
Roosevelt Av. Chat —2D 14
Ropemakers Ct. Chat —7E 8
Roper Clo. Gill —6C 16
Rope Wlk. Chat —3D 8
Roseacre Gdns. Bear —7F 31
Roseacre La. Bear —1F 37
Rosebery Clo. Sit —5H 21
Rosebery Rd. Chat —6C 8
Rosebery Rd. Gill —1H 9
Rose Cotts. Loose —7J 35 (off Old Loose Hill)
Rose Cotts. Roch —7D 2
Roseholme. Maid —2G 35
Roseleigh Av. Maid —7F 29
Roseleigh Rd. Sit —7B 20
Rosemary Clo. Chat —5D 14
Rosemary Rd. Bear —1F 37
Rosemary Rd. E Mal —2G 27
Rosemount Clo. Loose —1J 41
Rosemount Ct. Roch —6J 3
Rose St. Roch —5B 8
Rose Yd. Maid —7K 29
Rosslyn Grn. Maid —6E 28
Ross St. Roch —4B 8
Rother Ho. Maid —4C 36
Rother Vale. Chat —6G 15
Roundel, The. Sit —7D 20
Roundhay. Leyb —2E 26
Roundwell. Bear —7J 31
Rover Rd. Chat —7F 15
Rowan Ho. Maid —1D 34
Rowan Lea. Chat —1F 15
Rowan Wlk. Chat —5C 8
Rowbrocke Clo. Gill —6D 16
Rowe Pl. Eccl —4H 23
Rowland Av. Gill —6J 9
Rowland Clo. Maid —1H 35
Royal Eagle Clo. Roch —1C 8
Royal Engineers Rd. S'lng —2H 29
Royal Sovereign Av. Chat —1F 9
Royal Star Arc. Maid —7J 29
Roydon Hall Rd. E Peck —7A 32
Royston Rd. Bear —1F 37
Roystons Clo. Gill —6F 11
Ruckinge Way. Gill —5C 10
Rudge Clo. Chat —7H 15
Rugby Clo. Chat —5D 14
Rumwood Ct. Langl —7H 37
Running Horse Roundabout. S'lng —2H 29
Runnymede Gdns. Maid —4K 35
Rush Clo. Chat —6E 14
Rushdean Rd. Roch —3F 7
Rushmead Dri. Maid —5K 35
Ruskin Clo. E Mal —3G 27
Russell Clo. Sit —6A 20
Russell Ct. Chat —5F 9
Russell Rd. Ayle —3B 24
Russell's Av. Gill —1G 17
Russet Clo. Roch —7G 3
Russet Ct. Cox —2F 41
Russets, The. Maid —6E 28
Russett Clo. Ayle —3B 28
Russet Way. King H —2A 32
Ruth Ho. Maid —6H 29
Rutland Cotts. Leeds —7K 37
Rutland Pl. Gill —6C 16
Rutland Way. Maid —4D 36
Ryarsh La. W Mal —2C 26
Rycault Clo. Maid —1H 35
Rycaut Clo. Gill —6D 16
Rydal Ho. Maid —5C 36
Ryde Clo. Chat —1F 15
Ryegrass Clo. Chat —3G 15

Sabre Ct. Gill B —7A 10
Saddlers Clo. Weav —6D 30
Sadlers Clo. Chat —7B 14
Saffron Way. Chat —4D 14
Saffron Way. Sit —2D 20
Sail Field Ct. Chat —1D 8
Sailmakers Ct. Chat —6F 9
St Albans Clo. Gill —1J 9
St Alban's Rd. Roch —2F 7
St Alban Wlk. Chat —5C 8
St Andrew's Clo. Barm —2D 34
St Andrews Ho. Maid —1D 34
St Andrews Rd. Gill —1H 9
St Andrew's Rd. Maid —2D 34
St Anne Ct. Maid —7H 29
St Asaph Ho. Maid —5C 36
St Barnabas Clo. All —3F 29
St Barnabas Clo. Gill —5H 9
St Bartholomews La. Roch —4C 8
St Bartholomews Ter. Roch —4C 8
St Benedict Rd. Snod —3A 22
St Catherines Hospital. Roch —4B 8
St Clements Ho. Roch —3B 8
St Edmunds Way. Gill —7G 11

A-Z Maidstone, Chatham, Gillingham & Rochester 53

St Faith's La.—Stratford La.

St Faith's La. Bear —7G 31
St Faith's St. Maid —7J 29
St George's Rd. Gill —2G 9
St George's Sq. Maid —1G 35
St Helen's Cotts. Maid —4B 34
St Helens La. E Far —4B 34
St Helier's Clo. Maid —2E 34
St James Clo. E Mal —3G 27
St John's Av. Sit —6F 21
St John's Clo. High —3E 2
St John's Rd. Gill —5G 9
St John's Rd. High —3E 2
St Johns Rd. Hoo —1H 5
St Johns Way. Roch —6J 7
(in two parts)
St Katherine's La. Snod —3B 22
St Laurence Av. Maid —3E 28
St Lawrence Clo. Bap —7H 21
St Leonards Av. Chat —6D 8
St Leonards Rd. Ail —3F 29
St Leonard's St. W Mal —5B 26
St Lukes Av. Maid —6A 30
St Lukes Rd. Maid —6A 30
St Margarets Bank. Roch —4B 8
St Margarets Banks. Roch —3B 8
St Margaret's Clo. Maid —2E 34
St Margarets Dri. Gill —4C 16
St Margaret's M. Roch —3A 8
St Margaret's St. Roch —4K 7
St Mark's Clo. N'tn —2E 18
St Marks Ct. Eccl —4H 23
St Mark's Ho. Gill —3G 9
St Martin's Clo. Det —2F 31
St Martin's Clo. N'tn —2E 18
St Mary's Ct. W Mal —3C 26
St Mary's Gdns. Chat —1F 9
St Mary's Rd. Gill —2G 9
St Mary's Rd. Roch —1K 7
St Mary's View. N'tn —2E 18
St Mary's Wlk. Burh —1H 23
St Matthew's Clo. N'tn —2E 18
St Matthews Dri. Roch —6J 7
St Michael's Clo. Ayle —7A 24
St Michaels Clo. Chat —5D 8
St Michaels Clo. Sit —5D 20
St Michaels Ct. Strood —7K 3
St Michael's Rd. Maid —1G 35
St Michael's Rd. Sit —5C 20
(in two parts)
St Nicholas Gdns. Roch —1H 7
St Paul's Clo. Roch —3F 7
St Paul's St. Sit —4C 20
(in two parts)
St Peter's Bri. Maid —7J 29
St Peter's Clo. Dit —2J 27
St Peter's Ct. Dit —2J 27
St Peter's Path. Roch —3A 8
St Peter's Pl. Eccl —4H 23
St Peter's Rd. Dit —2J 27
St Peter St. Maid —6J 29
St Peter St. Roch —4B 8
St Philip's Av. Maid —1A 36
St Saviours Rd. Maid —6C 36
St Stephen's Clo. N'tn —2E 18
St Stephen's Cotts. Maid —6B 34
St Stephens M. Roch —1C 14
St Stephen's Sq. Maid —2H 35
St Werburgh Ct. Hoo —2H 5
St Werburgh Cres. Hoo —2H 5
St Werburgh Ter. Hoo —2J 5
St William's Way. Roch —5B 8
Salem St. Maid —1K 35
Salisbury Av. Gill —1D 16
Salisbury Clo. Sit —5G 21
Salisbury Ho. Maid —5C 36
Salisbury Rd. Blue B —2B 24
Salisbury Rd. Chat —5E 8
Salisbury Rd. Maid —5K 29
Sally Port. Gill —2E 8
Sally Port Gdns. Gill —2E 8
Saltings Rd. Snod —3C 22
Salts Av. Loose —2J 41
Salts Farm Cotts. Maid —1K 41
Salts La. Loose —7K 35
Saltwood Rd. Maid —3J 35
Samara Clo. Chat —1E 24
Samphire Clo. Weav —7D 30
Sanctuary Rd. Gill —5A 10
Sandbourne Dri. Maid —2J 29
Sandford Rd. Sit —4K 19
Sandgate Ct. Gill —5F 17
Sandhill La. High —1F 3
Sandhurst Clo. Gill —5C 10
Sandling Ct. Maid —4A 30
Sandling La. S'lng —1H 29
(in two parts)
Sandling Rd. Maid —4J 29
(in two parts)
Sandling Way. St Mi —6F 5
Sandown Dri. Gill —2D 16
Sandown Rd. W Mal —3C 26
Sandpiper Rd. Chat —7H 15
Sandringham Rd. Gill —5E 16
Sandstone Rise. Chat —2G 25
Sandycroft Rd. Roch —6H 3
Sandy Dell. Hem —6A 16
Sandy La. Bear —6G 31
Sandy La. Boxl —2B 30
Sandy La. Snod —4A 22
Sandy La. W Mal —2B 26
Sandy Mt. Bear —6G 31
Sappers Wlk. Gill —3G 9
Saracen Clo. Gill B —7A 10
Saracen Fields. W'slde —2G 25
Sarsen Heights. Chat —1D 24
Sassoon Clo. Lark —6C 22
Satis Av. Sit —2C 20
Saunders St. Chat —5D 8
Saunders St. Gill —2G 9
Savage Rd. Chat —6F 15
Sawyers Ct. Chat —6F 9
Saxon Clo. King H —2A 32
Saxon Clo. Roch —6H 3
Saxon Pl. Roch —3H 7
Saxons Dri. Maid —4A 30
Saxon Shore Way. Gill —1A 10
Saxton St. Gill —3G 9
Scarborough La. Burh —1E 22
Scarlett Clo. Chat —4G 15
Scholars Rise. Roch —1F 7
Scholey Clo. Hall —5D 12
School Av. Gill —4J 9
School La. Bap —6H 21
School La. B'den —5H 19
School La. High —4E 2
School La. Maid —3D 36
School La. N'tn —2D 18
School La. Sut V —6K 43
School Rd. Sit —6F 21
School Rd. Woul —4E 12
School Vs. Nett —7E 32
Schreiber M. Gill —3H 9
Scimitar Clo. Gill B —7A 10
Scotby Av. Chat —5F 15
Scott Av. Gill —1G 17
Scott Clo. Dit —3K 27
Scotteswood Av. Chat —6D 8
Scott's Ter. Chat —5D 8
Scott St. Maid —5J 29
Scraces Cotts. Maid —4D 34
Scragged Oak Cvn. Pk. Det —1G 31
Scragged Oak Rd. Det —1G 31
Scrubbs La. Maid —7G 29
Seaford Ct. Roch —4K 7
Seagull Rd. Roch —2E 6
Sealand Ct. Roch —4K 7
Seamew Ct. Roch —1E 6
Seaton Rd. Gill —5J 9
Seaview Rd. Gill —4G 9
Second Av. Chat —7F 9
Second Av. Gill —5J 9
Secretan Rd. Roch —7K 7
Segrete Cres. Chat —5C 14
Sedley Clo. Ayle —1C 28
Sedley Clo. Gill —6C 16
Sefton Rd. Chat —3G 15
Selbourne Rd. Gill —1H 9
Selbourne Wlk. Maid —6E 36
Selby Rd. Maid —1E 42
Sellinge Grn. Gill —5C 10
Selstead Clo. Gill —7C 10
Semple Gdns. Chat —5C 8
Senacre La. Maid —6D 36
Senacres Cotts. Maid —6E 36
Senacre Sq. Maid —5E 36
Sessions Ho. Sq. Maid —6J 29
Settington Av. Chat —7G 9
Severn Rd. Chat —4G 15
Sevington Pk. Maid —6J 35
Sextant Pk. Roch —2C 8
Seymour Rd. Chat —5F 9
Seymour Rd. Rain —1J 17
Seymour's Cotts. Leeds —6K 37
Shackleton Clo. Chat —3F 15
Shades, The. Roch —1D 6
Shaftesbury Clo. E Mal —2G 27
Shaftesbury Dri. Maid —7F 29
Shakespeare Rd. Gill —4G 9
Shakespeare Rd. Sit —5E 20
Shamel Bus. Cen. Roch —1A 8
Shamley Rd. Chat —7H 15
Shanklin Clo. Chat —1G 15
Sharfleet Dri. Roch —1D 6
Sharnal La. Snod —3C 22
Sharon Cres. Chat —5D 14
Sharsted Way. Bear —6G 31
Sharsted Way. Hem —6A 16
Shawstead Rd. Gill —2G 15
Shaws Way. Roch —5A 8
Shaws Wood. Roch —6K 3
Sheal's Ct. Maid —2K 35
Sheal's Cres. Maid —2K 35
Shearers Clo. Weav —7D 30
Shearwater. Maid —6E 28
Shearwater Clo. Roch —1E 6
Sheldon Dri. Gill —1F 17
(in two parts)
Sheldon Way. Lark —7C 22
Shelley Rd. Maid —2F 35
Shenley Gro. S'lng —1J 29
Shepherds Ga. Hem —4K 15
Shepherds Ga. Dri. Weav —6D 30
Shepherds Way. Langl —1K 43
Shepperton Clo. Chat —5G 15
Sheppey Rd. Maid —5J 35
Sheppey Way. Bob —4J 19
Shepway Ct. Maid —4B 36
Sheraton Ct. Chat —1D 24
Sherbourne Dri. Maid —2E 34
Sherbourne Dri. Strood —6J 3
Sheridan Clo. Chat —2G 15
Sheridan Clo. Maid —3H 29
Sheridan Ct. Roch —6J 7
Sheriff Dri. Chat —7E 14
Sherman Clo. Gill —7B 10
Shernolds. Maid —5A 36
Sherwood Av. Chat —7E 14
Sherwood Ho. Chat —6D 14
Shillingheld Clo. Bear —6E 30
Shingle Barn La. W Far —2A 40
Ship La. Roch —4C 8
Shipley Ct. Maid —7K 29
Shipwrights Av. Chat —7E 8
Shirley Av. Chat —4B 14
Shirley Ct. Maid —7D 36
Shirley Way. Bear —1F 37
Sholden Rd. Roch —6A 4
Shorefields. Rain —6G 11
Shoreham Wlk. Maid —5E 36
Shorland Ct. Roch —4K 7
Shortlands Grn. Maid —7E 36
Shortlands Rd. Sit —5E 20
Short La. Gill —2A 10
Short St. Chat —5F 9
Shorts Way. Roch —5J 7
Shottenden Rd. Gill —1H 9
Shropshire Ter. Maid —5D 36
Shrubsole Dri. S'lng —7D 24
Shurland Av. Sit —7D 20
Sidney Rd. Gill —1G 9
Sidney Rd. Roch —6J 7
Sidney St. Maid —2F 35
Signal Ct. Gill —7F 11
Silchester Ct. Maid —4B 30
Silverbank. Chat —3E 14
Silver Birches. Chat —6E 14
Silverdale. Maid —2C 34
Silverdale Dri. Gill —2F 17
Silverdale Gro. Sit —6A 20
Silver Hill. Chat —5D 8
Silver Hill. Roch —6H 7
Silver Hill Gdns. Chat —5D 8
Silverspot Clo. Rain —2F 17
Silver Tree Clo. Chat —1E 24
Silverweed Rd. Chat —5C 14
Simmonds La. Otham —6G 37
Simpson Rd. Sit —4A 20
Simpson Rd. Snod —4C 22
Sinclair Clo. Gill —5E 16
Sindal Shaw Ho. Chat —5C 14
Sindals La. Chat —1J 25
Singapore Dri. Gill —3E 8
Sir Evelyn Rd. Roch —7K 7
Sir Hawkins Way. Chat —4D 8
Sir Thomas Longley Rd. Roch —2C 8
Siskin Wlk. Lark —1G 27
Sissinghurst Dri. Maid —7E 28
Sittingbourne Ind. Est. Sit —4D 20
Sittingbourne Rd. Det & S'bry —1J 31
Sittingbourne Rd. Maid —6A 30
(in two parts)
Skene Clo. Gill —7G 11
Skinners Clo. Eccl —4J 23
Skinner St. Chat —5D 8
Skinner St. Gill —3G 9
(in two parts)
Skinners Way. Langl —1K 43
Skua Ct. Roch —1E 6
Skye Clo. Maid —5K 35
Slade Clo. Chat —7F 15
Slatin Rd. Roch —7K 3
Slicketts Hill. Chat —4E 8
Small Profits. Yald —7G 33
Smarts Cotts. Bear —7H 31
Smeed Clo. Sit —5F 21
Smeed Dean Cen. Sit —5E 20
Smetham Gdns. Roch —6K 3
Smith Rd. Chat —6F 15
Smiths Est. S'lng —7C 24
Smith's Hill. W Far —7K 33
Smith St. Roch —2J 7
Snipe Ct. Roch —1E 6
Snodhurst Av. Chat —4C 14
Snodhurst Ho. Chat —2D 14
Snodland By-Pass. Snod —5B 22
Snowdon Av. Maid —6A 30
Snowdon Clo. Chat —2F 15
Snowdon Pde. Maid —6B 30
Solent Gdns. Chat —1F 15
Solomon Rd. Gill —7F 11
Solomon's Rd. Chat —4D 8
Somerfield Clo. Maid —7G 29
Somerfield La. Maid —6G 29
Somerfield Rd. Maid —7G 29
Somerset Clo. Chat —1G 15
Somerset Clo. Sit —5A 20
Somerset Rd. Maid —4B 36
Somner Wlk. Maid —1E 42
Sorrell Rd. Chat —5C 14
Sortmill Rd. Snod —3D 22
South Av. Gill —6A 10
South Av. Sit —6E 20
S. Aylesford Retail Pk. Ayle —3B 28
South Bank. Sut V —6K 43
Southbourne Gro. Chat —5E 14
S. Bush La. Gill —4H 17
South Ct. Maid —3K 35
South Cres. Cox —2F 41
S. Eastern Rd. Roch —1A 8
Southey Way. Lark —6B 22
Southfields. Roch —5K 7
Southill Rd. Chat —5D 8
South La. Sut V —7K 43
South Pk. Bus. Village. Maid —3K 35
South Pk. Rd. Maid —3A 36
South Rd. Chat —1F 9
(Officers' Rd.)
South Rd. Chat —1E 8
(Wood St.)
S. Side Three Rd. Chat —7F 5
South St. Barm —3B 34
South View. Bear —7H 31
Southwark Rd. Roch —2F 7
South Ways. Sut V —6K 43
Southwell Rd. Roch —2E 6
Southwood. Maid —2C 34
Sovereign Boulevd. Chat —6J 9
Sovereign Ct. Roch —2E 6
Sovereigns, The. Maid —7G 29
Spade La. H'lip —4J 17
Spearhead Rd. Maid —4J 29
Spectrum Bus. Cen. Roch —7C 4
Spectrum Bus. Est. Maid —1E 42
Spectrum W. Maid —3G 29
Speedwell Av. Chat —5C 14
Speedwall Clo. Gill —3J 9
Speedwell Clo. Weav —7D 30
Spekes Rd. Hem —3B 16
Speldhurst Ct. Maid —7G 29
Spencer Clo. Chat —4E 14
Spencer Flats. Chat —1F 15
Spencer Way. Maid —5D 36
Spenlow Dri. Chat —1E 24
Spiers, The. Gill —3C 10
Spillway, The. Maid —2G 35
Spindle Glade. Maid —6B 30
Spindlewood Clo. Chat —6F 15
Spinnaker Ct. Roch —7A 8
Spinney, The. Maid —2A 36
Spires, The. Maid —7G 29
Spires, The. Roch —3F 7
Spitfire Clo. Chat —3F 15
Spitfire Rd. W Mal —1A 32
Sportsfield. Maid —6A 30
Sportsmans Cotts. King H —6C 26
Spot Farm Cotts. Maid —5J 37
Spot La. Down —2E 36
(in three parts)
Sprig, The. Bear —7F 31
Spring Cotts. Lin —7G 41
Springett Clo. Eccl —4H 23
Springett Way. Cox —1G 41
Springfield Av. Maid —4J 29
Springfield Rd. Gill —2J 9
Springfield Rd. Lark —7B 22
Springfield Rd. Sit —4B 20
Springfield Ter. Chat —4D 8
Springvale. Gill —3C 16
Spring Vale. Maid —7H 29
Springwood Clo. Maid —1C 34
Springwood Rd. Barm —1D 34
Sprotshill Clo. Sit —3C 20
Spruce Clo. Lark —1H 27
Spurgeon's Cotts. Langl —3H 41
Spurway. Bear —7F 31
Sqaure Hill. Maid —7A 30
Square Hill Rd. Maid —1A 36
Square, The. Hunt —6A 40
Squires Clo. Roch —1D 6
Stable Clo. Chat —4G 15
Stable Cotts. Maid —5F 35
Staceys St. Maid —6J 29
Staffa Rd. Maid —5K 35
Stafford St. Gill —3F 9
Stag Rd. Chat —4G 15
Stagshaw Clo. Maid —2K 35
Stake La. Hall —3C 12
Stalham Ct. Hem —5B 16
Stalin Av. Chat —1F 15
Stampers, The. Maid —2G 35
Standen Clo. Gill —5E 16
Stanford Dri. Maid —1F 35
Stanford Way. Cux —6E 6
Stanhope Av. Sit —6D 20
Stanhope Clo. Maid —4H 29
Stanhope Rd. Roch —1J 7
Stanley Rd. Chat —3G 15
Stanley Rd. Gill —2G 9
Stansted Clo. Maid —4F 29
Staple Clo. Sit —4C 20
Staplehurst Rd. Gill —5B 10
Staplehurst Rd. Sit —5A 20
Staplers Ct. Maid —3A 30
Star Hill. Roch —3B 8
Star La. Gill —1K 15
Star Mill Ct. Chat —6H 9
Star Mill La. Chat —6H 9
Starnes Ct. Maid —6K 29
Station App. Hall —4C 12
Station App. Maid —1J 35
Station Hill. E Far —5D 34
Station Hill Cotts. Maid —5E 34
Station Rd. Cux —6E 6
Station Rd. Dit —2K 27
Station Rd. H'shm —6K 39
Station Rd. Maid —6J 29
Station Rd. N'tn —3D 18
Station Rd. Rain —1F 17
Station Rd. Strood —7K 3
Station St. Sit —5C 20
Steadman Clo. High —2E 2
Steele St. Roch —7J 3
Steelfield Ind. Est. Gill —1K 9
Steerforth Clo. Roch —6A 8
Stephens Pl. Maid —3H 35
Step Style. Sit —7F 21
Sterling Av. Maid —6F 29
Sterling Rd. Sit —7B 20
Stevens Clo. Snod —2C 22
Stevenson Clo. Maid —1J 35
Stevenson Way. Lark —6B 22
Stevens Rd. Eccl —4H 23
Stewart Ho. Chatt —1C 4
Stickens La. E Mal —5F 27
Stilebridge La. Lin —7K 41
Stirling Clo. Gill —5E 16
Stirling Clo. Roch —5J 7
Stirling Rd. W Mal —1A 32
Stockbury Dri. Maid —4G 29
Stockett La. Cox & E Far —2F 41
Stockton Clo. Maid —3A 30
Stoke Rd. Hoo —2J 5
Stoke Rd. Bus. Cen. Hoo —2J 5
Stoneacre Clo. Gill —4D 16
Stoneacre Cotts. Maid —5H 37
Stoneacre La. Otham —4G 37
Stone Cotts. E Far —5C 34
Stone Cotts. Langl —1G 43
Stone Cotts. Maid —3C 36
Stonecross Lea. Chat —7G 9
Stonehorse Ct. Roch —4J 3
Stonehorse La. Roch —4J 3
Stoney Hill. Chat —5F 9
Stony La. Roch —4K 13
Stopford Rd. Gill —4G 9
Stour Clo. Roch —1H 7
Stour Ho. Maid —4C 36
Strand App. Rd. Gill —1J 9
Stratford Av. Gill —1D 16
Stratford La. Gill —1F 17

54 A-Z Maidstone, Chatham, Gillingham & Rochester

Stratford Rd.—Waterside Ct.

Stratford Rd. W Mal —3B 26
Straw Mill Hill. Maid —3H 35
Stream Cotts. S'lng —2H 29
Streamside. Dit —2J 27
Stream, The. Dit —2K 27
Street End Rd. Chat —1F 15
Street Farm Cotts. Hoo —1K 5
Streetfield Rd. Gill —7F 11
Street, The. Bap —6H 21
Street, The. Bear —7H 31
Street, The. B'den —7J 19
Street, The. Boxl —1B 30
Street, The. Bred —7B 16
Street, The. Det —2F 31
Street, The. H'lip —5K 17
Street, The. Shorne —4A 2
Street, The. Tstn —5H 33
Street, The. Up H'lng —5A 12
Strover St. Gill —1G 9
Stuart Clo. Maid —5A 30
Stuart Rd. Gill —5H 9
Sturdee Av. Gill —4J 9
Sturdee Cotts. Hoo —1K 5
Sturla Rd. Chat —6E 8
Sturmer Ct. King H —2B 32
Sturry Way. Gill —6C 10
Style Clo. Gill —5E 16
Styles La. Boxl —7G 25
Suffolk Av. Gill —7F 11
Suffolk Ct. Gill —7F 11
Suffolk M. Chat —4D 8
Suffolk Rd. Maid —4C 36
Sugarloaf Hill. Chat —6H 9
Sultan Rd. Chat —1G 25
Sunderland Dri. Rain —1G 17
Sunderland Quay. Roch —2B 8
Sundridge Dri. Chat —5E 14
Sundridge Hill. Cux —5E 6
Sunerland Clo. Roch —5J 7
Sunningdale Clo. Gill —3D 16
Sunningdale Ct. Maid —7A 30
Sunningdale Dri. Gill —3D 16
Sunny Bank. Murs —4F 21
Sunnyfields Clo. Gill —1E 16
Sunnymead Av. Gill —3J 9
Sunnyside. Bear —7H 31
(off Street, The)
Sun Ter. Chat —5F 15
Superabbey Est. Ayle —1E 28
Surrey Rd. Maid —4C 36
Sussex Dri. Chat —5E 14
Sussex Rd. Maid —3C 36
Sutherland Gdns. Gill —3E 16
Sutton Clo. Rain —1G 17
Sutton Rd. Maid —4A 36
Sutton St. Bear —1J 37
Sutton Valence Hill. Sut V —6K 43
Swain Clo. Roch —7H 3
Swain Rd. Gill —3B 16
Swale Ho. Sit —5E 20
Swallow Rise. Chat —4E 14
Swallow Rd. Lark —1G 27
Swan Clo. Sit —5F 21
Swanstree Av. Sit —7F 21
Swan St. W Mal —3D 26
Sweets La. E Mal —7H 27
Swift Clo. Lark —1H 27
Swift Cres. Chat —3F 15
Swiller's La. Shorne —4A 2
Swingate Clo. Chat —7F 15
Swinton Av. Chatt —1D 4
Sycamore Cres. Maid —6F 29
Sycamore Dri. Ayle —2B 28
Sycamore Rd. Roch —3G 7
Sydney Av. Sit —5A 20
Sydney Rd. Chat —5E 8
Sylewood Clo. Roch —1K 13
Sylvan Glade. Chat —2E 24
Sylvan Rd. Gill —1C 16
Sylvestre Clo. Hall —5C 12
Symmonds Dri. Sit —3F 21
Symons Av. Chat —6D 8

Tadburn Grn. Chat —5F 15
Taddington Wood La. Chat —7C 14
Taillour Clo. Kem —2D 20
Tail Race, The. Maid —2H 35
Talbot Rd. Maid —5F 29
Tamar Dri. Roch —2H 7
Tamar Ho. Maid —4D 36
Tamarind Clo. Hem —5A 16
Tanglewood Clo. Gill —3C 16
Tangmere Clo. Gill —3K 9
Tanker Hill. Gill —3D 16
Tannery Ct. Sit —4C 20
(off kings Mill Clo.)
Tanyard Cotts. Shorne —6A 2
Tanyard Hill. Shorne —5A 2
Target Bus. Cen. Maid —1F 43
Tasker Clo. Bear —1G 37
Tassell Clo. E Mal —2H 27
Taswell Rd. Gill —7G 11
Tatler Clo. Chat —7H 15
Tatsfield Clo. Gill —6A 10
Taunton Clo. Maid —6E 36
Taverners Rd. Gill —2D 16
Tavistock Clo. Chat —1D 24
Tavistock Clo. Gill —2E 16
Tavistock Clo. Sit —5B 20
Tay Clo. Chat —4F 15
Taylor's La. High —2E 2
Taylor's La. Roch —1K 7
Teal Cres. St Mi —6F 5
Teapot La. Ayle —1B 28
Teasaucer Hill. Maid —4J 35
Teasel Clo. Weav —7E 30
Teasel Rd. Chat —5D 14
Tedder Av. Chat —2E 14
Tees Ho. Maid —6D 36
Telegraph Hill. High —5E 2
Temeriare Mnr. Gill —2E 8
(off Middle St.)
Temperance Row. Woul —5E 12
Tempest Rd. W Mal —1A 32
Temple Ct. Maid —7J 29
Temple Gdns. Roch —2H 7
Temple Gdns. Sit —7F 21
Temple Ind. Est. Roch —2K 7
Temple St. Roch —1J 7
Temple Way. E Mal —3G 27
Ten Acre Ct. H'shm —7K 39
Ten Acre Way. Rain —6H 11
Tennyson Rd. Gill —5G 9
Tenterden Rd. Chat —4F 15
Terence Clo. Chat —6E 8
Terminus Rd. Maid —2D 34
Tern Cres. Roch —2E 6
Terrace Rd. Maid —7H 29
Terrace Rd. Sit —6F 21
Terrace, The. Chat —1D 8
Terrace, The. Roch —3A 8
Terry's Yd. Maid —7K 29
Terry Wlk. Leyb —1F 27
Test Ho. Maid —4D 36
Teston La. Tstn —5J 33
Teston Rd. W'bury —1E 32
Teston Rd. W Mal —4A 26
Teynham Grn. Gill —4A 10
Thackeray Rd. Lark —7B 22
Thames Av. Gill —1E 16
Thames Ho. Maid —4C 36
Thames View. Cli —1A 4
Thanet Ho. Maid —7E 36
Thanet Rd. Gill —5C 16
Thatchers, The. Maid —7E 28
Theodore Pl. Gill —3G 9
Third Av. Chat —7G 9
Third Av. Gill —5J 9
Thirlmere Clo. Gill —3A 10
Thirlmere Clo. Wain —6A 4
Thirsk Ho. Maid —6E 36
(off Fontwell Clo.)
Thistlebank. Chat —6E 14
Thistledown. Weav —7E 30
Thistledown Clo. Hem —5A 16
Thistle Wlk. Sit —4F 21
Thomas Rd. Sit —5F 21
Thomas St. Roch —5A 8
Thompson Clo. Rain —1G 17
Thomson Clo. Snod —1C 22
Thorn Clo. Chat —1B 24
Thorndale Clo. Chat —4B 14
Thorndike Clo. Chat —1D 14
Thorndike Ho. Chat —1D 14
Thornham Rd. Gill —5C 10
Thornhill Pl. Maid —5K 29
Thorn Wlk. Sit —4G 21
Thorold Rd. Chat —5F 9
Thorpe Wlk. Gill —6C 16
Thrale Way. Gill —5E 16
Threshers Dri. Weav —6C 30
Thrush Clo. Chat —2F 15
Thurlestone Ct. Maid —5J 29
Thurnham La. Bear —6G 31
Thurston Dri. Roch —1F 7
Tichborne Clo. Maid —5F 29
Tideway, The. Roch —2A 14
Tilbury Rd. Gill —6G 11
Tile Fields. Holl —2E 38
Tilghman Way. Snod —1D 22
Tilley Clo. Hoo —2H 5
Timberbank. Chat —3E 14
Timber Tops. Chat —2H 25
Tinker's All. Chat —1D 8
Tintagel Gdns. Roch —1H 7
Tintagel Mnr. Gill —2G 9
Tintern Rd. Maid —5F 29
Titchfield Clo. Maid —6E 36
Titchfield Rd. Maid —6E 36
Tobruk Way. Chat —3D 14
Todd Cres. Kem —1E 20
Toddington Cres. Chat —1B 24
Toledo Paddock. Gill —3H 9
Tolgate La. Roch —1K 7
Tollgate Way. S'lng —7C 24
Tom Joyce Clo. Snod —3B 22
Tonbridge Ct. Maid —1F 35
Tonbridge Rd. Maid —1H 35
Tonbridge Rd. Mere —4A 32
Tonbridge Rd. W'bury & Barm —5G 33
Tonge Rd. Sit —5F 21
Toronto Rd. Gill —4J 9
Tovil Grn. Maid —2H 35
Tovil Grn. Bus. Pk. Tovil —3G 35
Tovil Hill. Maid —3H 35
Tovil Rd. Maid —2J 35
Tower Gdns. Bear —7G 31
Tower La. Bear —7F 31
Tower View. King H —7C 26
Town Hill. W Mal —2D 26
Town Hill Clo. W Mal —2D 26
Town Rd. Cli —3J 3
Townsend Rd. Snod —1A 22
Tracies, The. N'tn —3E 18
Trafalgar Clo. Woul —4E 12
Trafalgar St. Gill —3G 9
Transom Ho. Roch —7A 8
Trapfield Clo. Bear —7H 31
Trapfield La. Bear —7H 31
(in two parts)
Trapham Rd. Maid —6G 29
Travertine Rd. Chat —1F 25
Trelawn Cres. Chat —7F 15
Trellyn Clo. Maid —2C 34
Trenton Clo. Maid —4E 28
Trent Rd. Chat —4F 15
Trevale Rd. Roch —7K 7
Trevino Dri. Chat —6D 14
Trewin Clo. Ayle —1A 28
Tribune Dri. Sit —3D 20
Trident Clo. Roch —1C 8
Trinity Ct. Ayle —7J 23
Trinity Rd. Gill —2G 9
(in two parts)
Trinity Rd. Sit —2D 20
Trinity Trad. Est. Sit —3D 20
Troodos Hill. Maid —3J 29
Trotts Hall Gdns. Sit —6D 20
Trotwood Clo. Chat —2E 24
Troutbeck Ho. Dit —2K 27
Troys Mead. Holl —2E 38
Trubridge Rd. Hoo —2H 5
Truro Clo. Gill —5D 10
Truro Ho. Maid —5C 36
Tudor Av. Maid —5A 30
Tudor Cotts. Maid —1H 41
Tudor Gro. Chatt —3D 4
Tudor Gro. Gill —1E 16
Tufa Clo. Chat —1F 25
Tufton Rd. Gill —7F 11
Tufton St. Maid —7K 29
Tumblers Hill. Sut V —6K 43
Tunbury Av. Chat —6D 14
Tunbury Av. S. Chat —1D 24
Tupman Clo. Roch —4K 7
Turgis Clo. Langl —1K 43
Turkey Ct. Maid —1B 36
Turner Clo. Kem —1D 20
Turnstone Rd. Chat —7G 15
Tuscan Dri. Chat —1G 25
Tutsham Farm. W Far —6J 33
20/20 Ind. Est. All —3F 29
Twisden Rd. E Mal —3G 27
Twogates Hill Cli —2H 3
Two Post All. Roch —2A 8
Twydall Grn. Gill —5B 10
Twydall La. Gill —6B 10
Twyford Clo. Gill —6G 11
Twyford Ct. Maid —5C 30
Tydeman Rd. Bear —2E 36
Tyland Cotts. S'lng —7C 24
Tyland La. S'lng —7C 24
Tyler Clo. E Mal —3G 27
Tyler Dri. Gill —5E 16
Tyne Clo. Chat —4G 15
Tyne Ho. Maid —6D 36
Typhoon Rd. W Mal —1A 32

Ufton Clo. Maid —3D 36
Ufton La. Sit —7C 20
Ulcombe Rd. Langl —2K 43
Ullswater Ho. Maid —5C 36
Ulundi Pl. Woul —4E 12
Undercliff. Maid —1J 35
Underdown Av. Chat —7D 8
Underwood Clo. Maid —2J 35
Unicumes La. Maid —2F 35
Union Pk. Bus. Cen. Maid —1E 42
Union Pl. Chat —4E 8
Union St. Chat —4E 8
Union St. Maid —7K 29
Union St. Roch —3A 8
Unity St. Sit —6C 20
Unwin Clo. Ayle —7J 23
Upbury Way. Chat —4E 8
Upchat Rd. Chatt —3C 4
Uplands Clo. Roch —2F 7
Upnor Rd. Upnor & Lwr U
(in two parts) —7B 4
Up. Barn Hill. Hunt —2B 40
Up. Britton Pl. Gill —3F 9
Up. Bush Rd. Cux —6B 6
Up. East Rd. Chat —7F 5
Up. Fant Rd. Maid —2F 35
Up. Field Rd. Sit —4F 21
Up. Hunton Hill. E Far —3D 40
Up. Luton Rd. Chat —5G 9
Upper Mill. W'bury —4E 32
Upper Rd. Maid —2A 36
Up. Stone St. Maid —1K 35
Upper St. Holl —1F 39
Upper St. Leeds —7A 38
Urquhart Clo. Chat —4E 14

Vale Dri. Chat —4B 14
Valence Ho. Maid —5B 36
Valenciennes Rd. Sit —6C 20
Valentine Clo. Gill B —7A 10
Valentine Rd. Maid —5D 36
Valerian Clo. Chat —6C 14
Vale Rd. Loose —1H 41
Valiant Rd. Chat —7G 15
Valley Dri. Maid —7J 35
Valley Rise. Chat —1D 24
Valley Rd. Gill —4J 9
Valley, The. Cox —2G 41
Valley View Rd. Roch —6K 7
Vancouver Dri. Gill —7C 10
Vange Cott. M. Roch —4K 7
Vanity La. Lin —4G 41
Varnes St. Eccl —4H 23
Vaughan Dri. Kem —1D 20
Vauxhall Cres. Snod —4B 22
Vectis Dri. Sit —1D 20
Veles Rd. Snod —2B 22
Ventnor Clo. Chat —1G 15
Vicarage Clo. Ayle —7H 23
Vicarage Clo. Hall —4C 12
Vicarage Ct. N'tn —2D 18
Vicarage La. E Far —6D 34
Vicarage La. Hoo —2J 5
Vicarage Rd. Gill —3G 9
Vicarage Rd. Sit —3B 20
Vicarage Rd. Strood —7K 3
Vicarage Row. High —3E 2
Vicary Way. Maid —6G 29
Victoria Clo. Chat —7B 14
Victoria Ct. Maid —1H 35
Victoria Dri. King H —3A 32
Victoria Pde. Maid —6J 29
Victoria Rd. Chat —6F 9
Victoria Rd. Sit —5B 20
Victoria Rd. W'slde —7B 14
(in two parts)
Victoria St. Eccl —4H 23
Victoria St. Gill —3G 9
Victoria St. Maid —1H 35
Victoria St. Roch —3B 8
Victoria St. Strood —1K 7
Victoria Ter. Roch —6J 7
Victory Mnr. Gill —1E 8
Victory Pk. Roch —1C 8
Vidgeon Av. Hoo —1G 5
View Rd. Cli —1K 3
Viking Clo. Roch —3H 7
Villa Rd. High —4D 2
Vincent Rd. Ayle —3A 24
Vincent Rd. Sit —6G 21
Vine Ct. W'bury —4F 33
Vineries, The. Gill —3J 9
Viners Clo. Sit —7C 20
Vines La. Roch —3A 8
Vineyard Cres. Gill —7H 11
Viney Cotts. Leeds —6A 38
Vinters Rd. Maid —6A 30
Vintners Ct. Weav —7D 30
Vintners Way. Weav —7D 30
Violet Clo. Chat —2E 24
Virginia Rd. Gill —1G 9
Vixen Clo. Chat —3G 15
Volante Dri. Sit —2C 20
Vulcan Clo. Chat —2F 15

Wadham Pl. Sit —7F 21
Waghorn Rd. Snod —2C 22
Waghorn St. Chat —6F 9
Wagoners Clo. Weav —7D 30
Wainscott Eastern By-Pass. Wain —5B 4
Wainscott Northern By-Pass. Strood & Wain —7C 2
Wainscott Rd. Wain —5B 4
Wainscott Wlk. Wain —4B 4
Wakefield Clo. Roch —2F 7
Wakehurst Clo. Cox —2E 40
Wakeley Rd. Rain —7G 11
Wake Rd. Roch —1A 14
Walderslade Cen. Chat —6E 14
Walderslade Rd. Chat —1D 14
Walderslade Village By-Pass. Chat —7D 14
Walderslade Woods. Chat —6B 14
Waldron Dri. Maid —7J 35
Wallace Rd. Roch —1C 14
Wallbridge La. Gill —5J 11
Wall Clo. Hoo —1H 5
Wallers Cotts. Maid —1C 40
Walleys Clo. Gill —7H 11
Wallis Av. Maid —7D 36
Wall, The. Sit —4C 20
Walmer Ct. Maid —6K 29
Walmer Gdns. Sit —4B 20
Walmers Av. High —3C 2
Walnut Clo. Chat —1F 15
Walnut Row. Dit —3J 27
Walnut Tree Av. Maid —7K 35
Walnut Tree Cotts. Maid —7K 35
Walnut Tree Ct. Lark —2J 27
Walnut Tree Dri. Sit —5B 20
Walnut Tree La. Maid —7K 35
Walpole Clo. E Mal —3G 27
Walsby Dri. Kem —1E 20
Walsham Ho. Maid —5K 29
Walsham Rd. Chat —1D 24
Walsingham Clo. Gill —6D 16
Walsingham Ho. Maid —5K 29
Walter Burke Av. Woul —4E 12
Walters Rd. Hoo —1J 5
Waltham Rd. Gill —5B 10
Warbler's Clo. Roch —1J 7
Warden Clo. Maid —7F 29
Warden Ct. Maid —7G 29
Warden Mill Clo. W'bury —5F 33
Warden Rd. Roch —5A 8
Warden Ter. W'bury —6E 32
(off Maidstone Rd.)
Warde's Cotts. Maid —4G 37
Wardwell La. Lwr Hal —2E 18
Warlingham Clo. Gill —7G 11
Warmlake Ind. Est. Sut V —4K 43
Warmlake Rd. Cha S —4G 43
Warner St. Chat —5D 8
Warnett Ct. Snod —1C 22
Warnford Gdns. Maid —4K 35
Warren Clo. Sit —7F 21
Warren La. H'lip —6J 17
Warren Rd. Blue B —2B 24
Warren Rd. S'fleet —5A 6
Warren View. Shorne —4A 2
Warren Wood Rd. Roch —2A 14
Warwick Cres. Roch —6H 7
Warwick Cres. Sit —4A 20
Warwick Pl. Maid —7H 29
Washington Ho. Maid —7D 36
Wateringbury Rd. E Mal —2G 33
Water La. H'shm —6H 39
Water La. Hunt —7A 40
Water La. Maid —7K 29
Water La. T'hm —7J 31
Water La. W Mal —3D 26
Waterloo Rd. Gill —4G 9
Waterloo Rd. Sit —4B 20
Waterloo St. Maid —1K 35
Waterlow Rd. Maid —5K 29
Watermeadow Clo. Hem —3K 15
Watermill Clo. Maid —6E 28
Water Mill Clo. Roch —7A 4
Waters Edge. Maid —2J 35
Waterside. Maid —6J 29
Waterside Ct. Leyb —7A 22
Waterside Ct. Roch —1C 8

A-Z Maidstone, Chatham, Gillingham & Rochester 55

Waterside La.—Zetland Av.

Waterside La. *Gill* —1K **9**
Waterside M. *W'bury* —6E **32**
Waters Pl. *Hem* —3A **16**
Waterworks Cotts. *Bear* —4E **30**
Waterworks Cotts. *Boxl* —7G **25**
Water Works Cotts. *Roch*
 —1J **13**
Watling Av. *Chat* —6H **9**
Watling Pl. *Sit* —6E **20**
Watling St. *Chat* —6H **9**
Watling St. *Strood* —7E **2**
Watson Av. *Chat* —4B **14**
Watsons Hill. *Sit* —4C **20**
Watts Almshouses. *Roch* —4A **8**
Watts Av. *Roch* —4A **8**
Watts Clo. *Snod* —2D **22**
Watts' St. *Chat* —5C **8**
Wat Tyler Way. *Maid* —7K **29**
Waveney Ho. *Maid* —4D **36**
Waverley Clo. *Chat* —7H **15**
Waverley Clo. *Cox* —3F **41**
Wayfield Rd. *Chat* —3D **14**
Waylands. *Bear* —7G **31**
Wayne Ct. *Roch* —5B **4**
Weald Clo. *Maid* —6B **36**
Weald Ct. *Sit* —7B **20**
Wealden St. *Chat* —5F **9**
Wealden Way. *Quar W* —4B **28**
Weatherly Clo. *Roch* —4A **8**
Weavering Clo. *Roch* —5K **3**
Weavering Cotts. *Weav* —1D **36**
Weavering St. *Weav* —1D **36**
Weavers, The. *Maid* —7E **28**
Webb Clo. *Hoo* —1H **5**
Webster Rd. *Gill* —7F **11**
Wedgewood Clo. *Maid* —6E **28**
Wedgewood Dri. *Chat* —2E **14**
Weeds Wood Rd. *Chat* —5D **14**
Week St. *Maid* —6K **29**
Weirton Hill. *Bou M* —6C **42**
Welcombe Ct. *Gill* —1D **16**
 (off Derwent Way)
Welland Ho. *Maid* —4D **36**
Well Cotts. *Det* —2F **31**
Weller Av. *Roch* —6B **8**
Wellington Ho. *Maid* —7D **36**
Wellington Pl. *Maid* —5J **29**
Wellington Rd. *Gill* —4G **9**
Wellington Rd. *Sit* —4K **19**
Wellington Way. *W Mal* —1A **32**
Well Rd. *Maid* —6K **29**
Wells Ct. *Roch* —3F **7**
Wells Ho. *Maid* —5C **36**
Wells Ho. *Sit* —5F **21**
Wells Rd. *Roch* —3F **7**
Well St. *E Mal* —5E **26**
Well St. *Loose* —2H **41**
Wellwinch Rd. *Sit* —4B **20**
Wemmick Clo. *Roch* —2B **14**
Wendover Clo. *Hall* —4D **12**
Wents, The. *Maid* —2D **40**
Went Woods. *Weav* —6E **30**
Wentworth Ct. *Sit* —4F **21**
Wentworth Dri. *Gill* —2E **16**
Wentworth Dri. *Sit* —4A **20**
Wesley Clo. *Maid* —1C **34**
Westbourne St. *Sit* —5C **20**
Westbrooke Clo. *Chat* —6E **8**
West Ct. *Maid* —3K **35**
Westcourt St. *Gill* —2E **8**
West Dri. *Chat* —4B **14**
Westergate Rd. *Roch* —6H **3**
Westerham Clo. *Maid* —6B **36**
Westerham Rd. *Sit* —6A **20**
Westerhill Rd. *Lin* —4F **41**
Western Rd. *Maid* —2F **35**

Westfield Bus. Cen. *Roch*
 —1A **8**
Westfield Sole Rd. *Chat* —2G **25**
Westlands Av. *Sit* —5K **19**
West La. *Sit* —5E **20**
 (Castle Rd.)
West La. *Sit* —5E **20**
 (East St.)
W. La. Trad. Est. *Sit* —4E **20**
W. Malling By-Pass. *W Mal*
 —5D **26**
W. Malling Ind. Est. *W Mal*
 —1A **26**
Westmarsh Clo. *Maid* —5E **36**
Westmead. *Lark* —6E **22**
W. Mill Rd. *Lark* —7E **22**
Westmorland Clo. *Maid* —5D **36**
Westmorland Grn. *Maid*
 —5D **36**
Westmorland Rd. *Maid* —5D **36**
Westmount Av. *Chat* —4D **8**
Weston Rd. *Roch* —1J **7**
West Pk. Rd. *Maid* —2A **36**
Westree Rd. *Maid* —1H **35**
Westree Rd. *Maid* —1H **35**
West Ridge. *Sit* —6B **20**
West Rd. *Chat* —6E **4**
 (Dock Head Rd.)
West Rd. *Chat* —1E **8**
 (Wood St.)
West St. *Gill* —2H **9**
West St. *H'shm* —6K **39**
West St. *Hunt* —6A **40**
West St. *Roch* —6K **3**
West St. *Sit* —5C **20**
 (in two parts)
West St. *W Mal* —3C **26**
W. View Cotts. *Cha S* —3H **43**
West Wlk. *Maid* —1E **34**
Westway. *Cox* —2F **41**
Westwood Rd. *Maid* —5K **35**
Westwood Wlk. *N'tn* —2D **18**
Wetheral Dri. *Chat* —5F **15**
Weybridge Clo. *Chat* —5G **15**
Wey Clo. *Chat* —4G **15**
Weyhill Clo. *Maid* —5B **30**
Wharf Rd. *Maid* —2H **35**
Wharf Way. *Sit* —4D **20**
Wheatcroft Clo. *Murs* —5F **21**
Wheatcroft Gro. *Gill* —2F **17**
Wheatear Way. *Chat* —2F **15**
Wheatfield. *Leyb* —2F **27**
Wheatfields. *Chat* —7H **15**
Wheatfields. *Weav* —7C **30**
Wheatsheaf Clo. *Maid* —4A **36**
Wheeler's La. *Lin* —1K **41**
Wheelers, The. *Gill* —3B **16**
Wheeler St. *Maid* —6K **29**
Wheeler St. Hedges. *Maid*
 —5A **30**
Whetynton Clo. *Roch* —2C **8**
Whiffen's Av. *Chat* —3D **8**
Whiffen's Av. W. *Chat* —3D **8**
Whimbrel Clo. *Sit* —1D **20**
Whimbrel Grn. *Lark* —1G **27**
Whimbrels, The. *St Mi* —6F **5**
Whimbrel Wlk. *Chat* —1G **25**
Whitchurch Clo. *Maid* —7H **29**
Whitcombe Clo. *Chat* —7G **15**
Whitebeam Dri. *Cox* —2E **40**
White Cotts. *S'lng* —2H **29**
Whitedyke Rd. *Snod* —7A **12**
White Ga. *Roch* —6H **3**
Whitegate Ct. *Gill* —4D **16**
Whitehall Rd. *Sit* —7C **20**

Whiteheads La. *Bear* —7G **31**
White Hill Rd. *Det* —7D **16**
Whitehorse Hill. *Chat* —5F **9**
White Horse La. *Otham* —6F **37**
Whitehouse Clo. *Hoo* —3J **5**
Whitehouse Cres. *Burh* —2J **23**
White Leaves Rise. *Cux* —6D **6**
White Rd. *Chat* —7E **8**
White Rock Ct. *Maid* —1H **35**
White Rock Pl. *Maid* —1H **35**
Whitewall Cen. *Roch* —7B **4**
Whitewall Rd. *Roch* —7B **4**
Whitewall Way. *Roch* —1B **8**
Whitmore St. *Maid* —5E **36**
Whittaker St. *Chat* —4E **8**
Wicken Ho. *Maid* —7F **29**
Wickens Pl. *W Mal* —3D **26**
Wickham Clo. *N'tn* —3D **18**
Wickham St. *Roch* —5B **8**
Widgeon Rd. *Roch* —2F **7**
Wierton Hill. *Bou M* —7C **42**
Wierton Rd. *Bou M* —4D **42**
Wigmore Rd. *Gill* —5B **16**
 (in two parts)
Wihtred Rd. *Bap* —7H **21**
Wilberforce Rd. *Cox* —2G **41**
Wildfell Clo. *Chat* —2G **25**
Wildman Clo. *Gill* —6D **16**
Wildwood Glade. *Hem* —5B **16**
Wilks Clo. *Rain* —6H **11**
Will Adams Ct. *Gill* —2G **9**
William Baker Ho. *Roy B*
 —3C **28**
William Rd. *Cux* —6E **6**
William St. *Gill* —7G **11**
William St. *Sit* —6C **20**
Willington Grn. *Maid* —5D **36**
Willington St. *Maid* —1E **36**
Willis Cotts. *Gill* —2K **25**
Willowby Gdns. *Gill* —5E **16**
Willow Cottage. *Hall* —3C **12**
Willow Ct. *Maid* —6B **35**
Willow Grange. *Hoo* —3H **5**
Willow Ho. *Chat* —5D **14**
Willow Ho. *Maid* —1D **34**
Willow Ho. *Sit* —6F **21**
Willow Industries. *S'lng* —7D **24**
Willowmead. *Leyb* —1F **27**
Willow Rise. *Down* —3E **36**
Willow Rd. *Lark* —7B **22**
Willow Rd. *Roch* —2G **7**
Willowside. *Snod* —1C **22**
Willows, The. *Gill* —6E **10**
Willows, The. *Kem* —1D **20**
Willows, The. *N'tn* —3D **18**
Willow Way. *Maid* —1A **36**
Wilmecote Ct. *Gill* —1D **16**
Wilmington Way. *Gill* —6B **10**
Wilson Av. *Roch* —7B **8**
Wilson Clo. *Maid* —5D **36**
Wilsons La. *E Far* —1D **40**
Wilton Dri. *Dit* —3J **27**
Wilton Ter. *Sit* —4K **19**
Wiltshire Clo. *Chat* —1G **15**
Wiltshire Way. *Maid* —4D **36**
Wimbourne Dri. *Gill* —3D **16**
Winchelsea Rd. *Chat* —3F **15**
Winchester Av. *Chat* —5D **14**
Winchester Ho. *Maid* —5C **36**
Winchester Pl. *Maid* —6K **29**
Winchester Way. *Gill* —7G **11**
Windermere Dri. *Gill* —2D **16**
Windermere Gro. *Sit* —6B **20**
Windermere Ho. *Maid* —5C **36**
Windmill Clo. *Roch* —6K **3**
Windmill Ct. *Langl* —2A **42**

Windmill Heights. *Bear* —7G **31**
Windmill La. Cvn. Site. *W Mal*
 —6B **26**
Windmill La. E. *W Mal* —5C **26**
Windmill La. W. *W Mal* —6C **26**
Windmill Rd. *Gill* —5F **9**
Windmill Rd. *Sit* —3B **20**
Windmill St. *Roch* —6K **3**
Windsor Av. *Chat* —6D **8**
Windsor Clo. *Maid* —5A **30**
Windsor Dri. *Sit* —7B **20**
Windsor Rd. *Gill* —3H **9**
Windward Rd. *Roch* —7A **8**
Windyridge. *Gill* —7J **9**
Wingham Clo. *Gill* —5C **10**
Wingham Clo. *Maid* —5E **36**
Wingrove Dri. *Strood* —7A **4**
Wingrove Dri. *Weav* —6D **30**
Winifred Rd. *Bear* —1E **36**
Winston Dri. *Wain* —5B **4**
Winston Rd. *Roch* —3F **7**
Winterfield La. *W Mal* —3F **27**
Wirrals, The. *Chat* —5E **14**
Wises La. *B'den* —6J **19**
Witham Way. *Roch* —1H **7**
Wittersham Clo. *Chat* —4F **15**
Wivenhoe Clo. *Rain* —6G **11**
Wodehouse La. *Lark* —6B **22**
Wolfe Rd. *Maid* —2E **34**
Wollaston Clo. *Gill* —6D **16**
Woodberry Dri. *Sit* —6F **21**
Woodbridge Dri. *Maid* —3H **35**
Woodbury Rd. *Chat* —1C **24**
Woodchurch Clo. *Chat* —4F **15**
Woodchurch Cres. *Gill* —6C **10**
Woodchurch Ho. *Gill* —6C **10**
Wood Clo. *Quar W* —3B **28**
Woodcourt Clo. *Sit* —7C **20**
Woodcut Cotts. *Holl* —2A **38**
Woodfield Way. *Chatt* —3B **4**
Woodford Rd. *Maid* —2E **34**
Woodgate La. *B'den* —7E **18**
Woodhurst. *Chat* —5B **14**
Woodhurst Clo. *Cux* —6D **6**
Woodland Clo. *W Mal* —3B **26**
Woodlands. *Chat* —7E **14**
Woodlands. *Cox* —2E **40**
Woodlands Av. *Snod* —2B **22**
Woodlands Clo. *Maid* —4K **29**
Woodlands Pde. *Dit* —3A **28**
Woodlands Rd. *Dit & Ayle*
 —2K **27**
Woodlands Rd. *Gill* —6K **9**
Woodlands Rd. *Sit* —6F **21**
Woodlands Ter. *Gill* —5K **9**
Woodland Way. *Maid* —4A **30**
Woodlea. *Leyb* —1G **27**
Woodleas. *Maid* —2C **34**
Woodpecker Glade. *Gill* —3D **16**
Woodpecker Rd. *Lark* —2G **27**
Woodruff Clo. *Bear* —1E **36**
Woodrush Pl. *St Mi* —6F **5**
Woodshole Cotts. *Iwade*
 —1B **20**
Woodside. *Gill* —3B **16**
Woodside Gdns. *Sit* —7B **20**
Woodside Rd. *Maid* —5B **36**
Woodstock Rd. *Roch* —1J **7**
Wood St. *Cux* —6D **6**
Wood St. *Gill* —1E **8**
Woodview Rise. *Roch* —6H **3**
Woodville Rd. *Maid* —2K **35**
Woolaston Clo. *Maid* —3J **35**
Woolbrook Clo. *Rain* —6H **11**

Woolett Rd. *Sit* —4A **20**
Woollett St. *Maid* —6K **29**
Woolley Rd. *Maid* —4D **36**
Woolwich Clo. *Chat* —2E **14**
Wootton Grn. *Gill* —5D **10**
Wopsle Clo. *Roch* —2B **14**
Worcester Av. *King H* —2B **32**
Worcester Clo. *Roch* —7G **3**
Worcester Dri. *Sit* —3B **20**
Worcester Rd. *Maid* —5C **36**
Wordsworth Clo. *Chat* —2G **15**
Wordsworth Rd. *Maid* —4A **30**
Wordsworth Way. *Lark* —6C **22**
Workhouse La. *E Far* —7F **35**
Wormdale Hill. *N'tn* —6D **18**
Wormdale Rd. *N'tn* —5C **18**
Wotton Clo. *Maid* —7D **36**
Wouldham Rd. *Roch* —1F **13**
Wrangleden Clo. *Maid* —7D **36**
Wrangleden Rd. *Maid* —7D **36**
Wren Clo. *Lark* —1G **27**
Wren Ind. Est. *Maid* —1E **42**
Wren's Cross. *Maid* —1K **35**
Wren Way. *Chat* —3F **15**
Wright Clo. *Gill* —6C **10**
Wyatt Ho. *Roch* —1J **7**
Wyatt Pl. *Roch* —1J **7**
Wyatt St. *Maid* —7K **29**
Wykeham Cotts. *Langl* —3J **41**
Wykeham Gro. *Leeds* —5B **38**
Wykeham Rd. *Sit* —5F **21**
Wykeham St. *Strood* —7K **3**
Wyke Mnr. Rd. *Maid* —7K **29**
Wylie Ho. *Chatt* —1D **4**
Wyles Rd. *Chat* —6C **8**
Wyles St. *Gill* —1G **9**
Wylie Ho. *Chatt* —1D **4**
Wylie Rd. *Hoo* —2H **5**
Wyllie Ct. *Sit* —2C **20**
Wyndham Rd. *Chat* —6C **8**
Wytherling Clo. *Bear* —6E **30**
Wyvern Clo. *Snod* —3C **22**
Wyvill Clo. *Gill* —4E **16**

Y
Yalding Clo. *Roch* —6K **3**
Yantlet Dri. *Roch* —1E **6**
Yarrow Ct. *Weav* —6E **30**
Yarrow Rd. *Chat* —5C **14**
Yaugher La. *H'lip* —7H **17**
Yeates Dri. *Kem* —1E **20**
Yelsted La. *Boxl* —3G **25**
Yelsted La. *Yel* —7G **17**
Yelsted Rd. *Yel* —7G **17**
Yeoman Ct. *Bear* —1G **37**
Yeoman Dri. *Gill* —7K **9**
Yeoman La. *Bear* —1G **37**
Yeoman Way. *Bear* —2F **37**
Yew Tree Clo. *Ayle* —2B **28**
Yew Tree Clo. *Chat* —1H **25**
Yew Tree Cotts. *Leeds* —6A **38**
Yew Tree Cotts. *S'lng* —2J **29**
Yewtree Ind. Est. *Ayle* —1A **28**
Yew Trees Ho. *Boxl* —1B **30**
Yoke Clo. *Roch* —7K **3**
York Av. *Chat* —6C **14**
York Av. *Gill* —4F **9**
York Hill. *Chat* —6G **9**
York Ho. *Maid* —5C **36**
York Rd. *Maid* —2A **36**
York Rd. *Roch* —5A **8**
Ypres Dri. *Kem* —1D **20**

Z
Zetland Av. *Gill* —6J **9**

Every possible care has been taken to ensure that the information given in this publication is accurate and whilst the publishers would be grateful to learn of any errors, they regret they cannot accept any responsibility for loss thereby caused.

The representation on the maps of a road, track or footpath is no evidence of the existence of a right of way.

The Grid on this map is the National Grid taken from the Ordnance Survey map with the permission of the Controller of Her Majesty's Stationery Office.

Copyright of Geographers' A-Z Map Co. Ltd.

No reproduction by any method whatsoever of any part of this publication is permitted without the prior consent of the copyright owners.